THE BOSTON
GENTLEMEN'S MOB

THE BOSTON
GENTLEMEN'S MOB

Maria Chapman and the Abolition Riot of 1835

Josh S. Cutler

THE
History
PRESS

Published by The History Press
Charleston, SC
www.historypress.com

Front cover, top: Maria Weston Chapman. *Boston Athenaeum*; *bottom*: "The Abolition Garrison in Danger & the Narrow Escape of the Scotch Ambassador. October 21, 1835." *Library Company of Philadelphia.*

First published 2021

Manufactured in the United States

ISBN 9781467150910

Library of Congress Control Number: 2021945865

For Charlie, Delilah, Jack and Connor

CONTENTS

CONTENTS

ACKNOWLEDGEMENTS

History is filled with pivot points we can look back on and recognize as significant, and the events of October 21, 1835, certainly qualify. It's been a pleasure diving into this subject matter to share this compelling story, and I'm grateful to everyone who helped along the way. That certainly includes my team of beta readers who shared valuable feedback and edits, especially Tom O'Brien, John Galluzzo, David Mittell Jr., Ben Cutler and Suzanne Cutler.

I'd also like to acknowledge the following individuals and organizations for their assistance: Marta Crilly and Meghan Pipp from the Boston City Archives; Rob MacLean and the staff at Weymouth's Tufts Library; Christopher Cantwell for assistance tracking down some key letters; Merlyn Liberty from Abington's Dyer Memorial Library; Kate Long and the Smith College Special Collections Department; Carolyn Ravenscroft and the Duxbury Rural and Historical Society; Leon Wilson and team from the Museum of African American History; Daniel Hinchen and the staff of the Massachusetts Historical Society; Diana Flemer, former chair of the Weymouth School Committee; and the staff at the Boston Athenaeum, Massachusetts State House Library, Boston Public Library, Historic New England and Harvard University's Houghton Library.

This is my second time publishing with The History Press. I am pleased to have worked with Mike Kinsella and their team of editors.

Thank you to Lori for all the love and support.

Part I

1835

MAYOR LYMAN: *Ladies, do you wish to see a scene of bloodshed, and confusion? If you do not, go home.*

MARIA CHAPMAN: *Mr. Lyman, your personal friends are the instigators of this mob; have you ever used your personal influence with them?*

MAYOR LYMAN: *I know no personal friends; I am merely an official. Indeed, ladies, you must retire. It is dangerous to remain.*

MARIA CHAPMAN: *If this is the last bulwark of freedom, we may as well die here, as anywhere.*

Maria Chapman, circa 1850. *American Magazine.*

Chapter 1

SUSAN PAUL

The rapid progress of the cause…will, ere long, annihilate the present corrupt state of things and substitute liberty and its concomitant blessings.

BOSTON, OCTOBER 21, 1835—There was no peace officer on site when Susan Paul arrived, only two grinning boys standing by the door who scampered off at her approach. It was shortly after two o'clock on a Wednesday afternoon, and Paul was joined by a handful of women in front of the antislavery office. The clippity-clop sound of hooves and the creak of carriage wheels rumbled past them on Washington Street.

The women expected trouble and cautiously entered the wood-framed building, climbing two flights of stairs to the lecture hall where the annual meeting of the Boston Female Anti-Slavery Society was to be held. Their meeting had already been postponed once. The original location was rejected by the building's owner after bowing to pressure from men of "property and standing" who opposed the society's abolitionist aims.

As Paul made her way upstairs, the passageway to the hall soon began to fill with unwelcome guests who cleaved to the walls and clogged up the way. The men hissed and heckled the women, and a few lobbed orange peel scraps their way. Some stood on the shoulders of others and glared over the partition—though none had yet dared breach the actual lecture hall where the meeting was to be held.

Reverend Thomas Paul. *Smithsonian.*

While the women greeted one another and settled in their seats, they sent a young boy downstairs to the street entrance to advise any late-arriving members that there was still room inside. Outside, it was an unseasonably warm October day, and inside tempers were also heated. Five more women pushed through and mounted the stairs, but many others turned away, unable—or unwilling—to confront the swarming crowd.

The lecture hall was arranged with plain wooden benches and a raised speaking platform. For Susan Paul, a seamstress and schoolteacher, the scene was reminiscent of a classroom. She took her seat along with her fellow

There are no known images of Susan Paul. Her sister Anne Paul Smith (*left*) died shortly after giving birth to her daughter, Susan Paul Smith (*right*), and Paul helped raise her. *UNC–Chapel Hill.*

members of the Boston Female Anti-Slavery Society as they awaited the arrival of their special guest. There were about twenty-five women in the room, most of them white—save Paul and a handful of others, including Lavinia Hilton and Julia Williams.

As its name announced, the society was avowedly antislavery, but until recently it had only included white women among its members. Despite being well-educated and "warmly loved and respected" by her fellow abolitionists, it was not until outside pressure was applied that Paul was invited to become a member.[1]

The issue had come to the fore when William Lloyd Garrison, publisher of the abolitionist newspaper the *Liberator*, was invited to speak shortly after the group's formation in the fall of 1833. Garrison saw the invitation as an opportunity to teach a lesson and declined. Instead, he urged the all-white women's society to engage in some self-reflection, declaring it "shocking to my feelings" that the members of an antislavery society would themselves be "slaves of a vulgar and insane prejudice."[2]

Garrison's message was heard "with respect," and the board agreed to his request. "I am happy to inform you that our decision was on the side of justice, that we resolved to receive our colored friends into our Society,

William Lloyd Garrison. *Boston Public Library.*

and immediately gave one of them a seat on our Board," they replied, referring to Susan Paul.[3] Thus, the society was now integrated, though equality remained elusive.

A PIONEERING FAMILY

Even before her formal admission, Susan Paul was a well-known figure in abolitionist circles. The granddaughter of an enslaved person, she hailed from a prominent and pioneering free Black family with strong ties to Garrison. Indeed, his letter was likely a not-so-subtle attempt to ensure Paul's selection for the board.

Susan Paul's grandfather Caesar Nero Paul had been enslaved as a teen and worked as a servant for a prominent New Hampshire merchant. Caesar Paul managed to get himself a rudimentary education and later served during the French and Indian Wars, which may have led to his manumission. By 1790, he lived as a free resident in the town of Stratham, New Hampshire, heading up a household of five. He must have been a strong believer in education because he sent all his sons to public schools near Exeter. Three of them later became Baptist ministers, including Susan's father, Thomas.

Thomas Paul grew up in New Hampshire and later moved to Boston. As a young man, he hosted religious meetings and led worshippers at Faneuil Hall. He was an accomplished orator—described as "dignified, urbane and attractive" in manner—and his congregation grew over time until the African Baptist Church, the city's first Black church, was officially organized in 1805 with Thomas Paul as the minister.[4]

Paul knew that his parishioners needed a permanent home, so he led efforts to build a church on Beacon Hill, which came to be known as the African Meeting House. During his career, Reverend Paul helped spearhead the growing movement of independent Black Baptist churches and traveled abroad to promote abolitionist aims and conduct missionary work. The African Meeting House, sometimes known as "Black Faneuil Hall," remained a spiritual, cultural and political center in Boston even after his death in 1831.

Susan Paul now carried her family's social reform mantel. In addition to her antislavery work, she was active with the local temperance society and women's rights movement. Two years prior, she was elected secretary of the Ladies Temperance Society, which had more than one hundred Black members and had recently helped lead a successful "cold water" campaign to encourage teetotalism.[5]

In the first edition of the *Liberator*, published on January 1, 1831, Garrison made clear that when it came to speaking out against slavery, he would pull no punches: "I *will be* as harsh as truth, and as uncompromising as justice. On this subject I do not wish to think, or speak, or write with moderation. No! No!…I am in earnest—I will not equivocate—I will not excuse—I will not retreat a single inch—AND I WILL BE HEARD." *New York Public Library.*

Within a few months, Garrison had changed the newspaper's masthead to the more familiar graphic. *Library Company of Philadelphia.*

Lately, she poured much of her energy into an innovative juvenile choir program for Black children in the city. The concerts featured a mix of patriotic songs and antislavery hymns sung by Paul's students, who ranged in age from four up to their early teens. The popular concerts served a dual purpose of highlighting the talents of the young children before mostly white audiences, while spreading the abolitionist message in verse. Paul also taught the students to read music and introduced them to classical composers. Occasionally, she also sang herself, sometimes performing with other antislavery society members, including Lavinia Hilton.

Despite her education, talents and status in the community ("I believe her to be very worthy, industrious and well informed," said one abolitionist), Paul was not immune to common racial prejudices. A recent trip out of the city for a choir performance before a local antislavery society had driven that point home. When it was time to leave for the event, three stately stagecoaches pulled up in front of Paul and her students, but when the hired drivers saw the complexions of the schoolchildren, they refused to offer them a ride. The men became enraged, shouting out racial epithets and proclaiming, "They would rather have their throats cut from ear to ear" than drive the students.[6]

For Paul, the episode was distressing but not unexpected. She was able to arrange alternative transportation, and the concert was held as scheduled. The choir was warmly received by a friendly abolitionist crowd, initially unaware of the "uncivil treatment" Paul and her students had overcome to get there. In a letter to Garrison shortly after the event, she shared details about the "cruel prejudice" she'd encountered but also sounded an optimistic note. "The rapid progress of the cause…will, ere long, annihilate the present corrupt state of things and substitute liberty and its concomitant blessings," she wrote.[7]

As Susan Paul settled into the wooden bench waiting for the meeting of the Boston Female Anti-Slavery Society to begin, she may not have realized how much her optimism would be tested on this day.

Chapter 2

MAYOR LYMAN

Behold, ye "Liberators," "Emancipators," "Abolitionists," the fruits of your extravagance and folly, your recklessness, and your criminal plots against the lives of your fellow-men!

Boston mayor Theodore Lyman was hurrying over to his chamber in the Old State House when he noticed a crowd gathering outside the antislavery office, or abolition room, as he called it. It was a warm afternoon, and he could smell the faint aroma of honey from a nearby fruit merchant mingling with pungent tobacco wafting from the reading room that shared space in his building.

The mayor had known for a few days that the women's antislavery society was hosting a meeting that afternoon, and rumors abounded that British abolitionist leader George Thompson was to be the featured speaker. Knowing that the presence of the contentious abolitionist could inflame local passions, the mayor had dispatched an assistant earlier in the day to see if the rumors were true.

When word came back that Thompson had left the city, the mayor breathed a sigh of relief. Under the circumstances, "no serious disturbance of the peace was to be feared," though he still took the precaution of having a few constables assembled.[8]

But now—Thompson or not—it appeared that trouble was brewing, so Mayor Lyman asked the city marshal to walk over and investigate. "I

was soon informed that the crowd was increasing very rapidly, and the society could not proceed in their business," he recalled, and he decided to march over to the antislavery office to judge for himself.[9] There was reason to be concerned.

"A Consummate Gentleman"

Mayor Theodore Lyman, circa 1820. *City of Boston Archives.*

Mayor Theodore Lyman, age forty-three and just shy of six feet tall, was a prominent figure in the city. Described as a "consummate gentleman," the handsome and well-dressed Lyman was first elected mayor two years earlier. His public persona could come across as formal and austere, but friends found him to be generous and warm-hearted. One prominent resident later said of Lyman that he was a man of "unusual grace of bearing and manly beauty." Another described him as "a model soldier, an admirable magistrate,…and a citizen of great public spirit."[10]

Lyman was a Latin and French scholar who, as a young man, studied at Exeter and Harvard and later in Europe. He authored several books and served as an officer in the Boston militia. His father, Theodore Lyman Sr., was a prosperous ship merchant who earned wealth trading furs and other goods with China.

Lyman's politics belied his patrician upbringing. Like his father, he grew up aligned with the Federalists but later found himself allied with the more populist Andrew Jackson. He even helped publish a newspaper dedicated to supporting Jackson's presidential candidacy, a move that put him at odds with the bulk of Boston's political ruling class.[11] When Lyman later ran successfully for mayor, he did so as a Jackson Democrat but drew support from rival political parties. It was no accident. In the intervening years, Lyman had grown distrustful of President Jackson and his Democratic Party, which he saw as drifting away from its reformist principles.[12]

Whether it was due to his consensus-building approach or convenient political elasticity, Mayor Lyman remained popular in the city of Boston. His prompt action in the wake of a deadly fire and anti-Catholic riot at a

The Old State House, circa 1835.
Historic New England.

nearby Charlestown convent the previous year was widely applauded, as were his frequent charitable acts and efforts to help the poor.

Still, it had been a challenging period for Mayor Lyman so far. In February, his oldest daughter, Julia, had died at the age of thirteen. And tensions in the city were rising over the issue of slavery.

The growing abolitionist movement, and especially the unyielding and uncompromising approach of antislavery advocates like Garrison, did not sit well with much of establishment Boston. Massachusetts had formally abolished slavery nearly a half century earlier, but many still benefited from the practice, directly or indirectly. The region's prosperous cotton textile industry in particular relied on raw cotton cultivated with the labor of enslaved persons. These mercantile relationships with the South, plus a general fear among the establishment that pressing hard on the issue of slavery could rupture the Union, fed the hostilities.

Mayor Lyman navigated a cautious and careful course. As a young state legislator, he had coauthored a report recounting the history of

slavery and rejecting efforts to limit the admission of free Black residents to Massachusetts, a state where he believed "civil and political toleration prevails."[13]

In the intervening years, the antislavery movement had progressed considerably with organized anti-enslavement societies and abolitionist newspapers springing up in Massachusetts, New York, Pennsylvania and elsewhere. Now, as Boston's mayor, Lyman faced a changing landscape, and his decisions did not always please abolitionists.

In June 1835, the mayor and the Boston City Council unanimously rejected a request by antislavery organizers to host a convention at Faneuil Hall.[14] "Rather ungenerous," one newspaper called the vote.[15] Garrison's paper, the *Liberator*, highlighted the decision on its front page and later called out Lyman by name, lumping him in among those "friends of Southern taskmasters." Garrison's admonishment adopted a mocking tone and even poked fun at Lyman's popularity in the city with a tongue-in-cheek reference to the "amiable and chivalrous" mayor.[16]

While the abolitionists fumed, most of Boston fiddled. Hostility to the antislavery cause was commonplace, and many were pleased to see the city rebuke these "advocates of abolition and disunion." Among them, the *Boston Commercial Gazette*, one of the leading abolitionist critics in the city: "They should not be permitted to profane old Faneuil Hall with doctrines, which if countenanced to any very considerable extent in New England…must inevitably lead to a dissolution of the Union."[17]

Whether Lyman's decision was rooted in opposition to the antislavery movement or just his appeasement of an uneasy electorate is unknown. Not long after, the city also rejected a request from a group of laborers seeking to host a public meeting at Faneuil Hall for the purpose of advocating for a ten-hour workday. In that case, some three hundred of the city's carpenters and masons decided to take to the streets instead. They assembled in front of the State House on a hot summer day in July to sing hymns and then paraded through Boston with banners to draw attention to their cause.[18]

Like the laborers, antislavery forces were not going away. In both cases, the city's decision to reject their chosen venue did little to silence their collective voice. On the contrary, the abolitionist movement was growing in intensity and inflaming passions on all sides—even in supposedly tolerant northern cities like Boston.

THE GREAT POSTAL CAMPAIGN

In the spring, abolitionist leaders in New York had launched what became known as the "Great Postal Campaign" to flood southern states with antislavery literature. It was an ambitious, organized and expensive effort designed to raise awareness and shape public opinion against slavery.[19]

The campaign certainly had an impact, and in some southern states, it was a violent one. In South Carolina, the transmission of these "diabolical materials" led to an attack on the mail.[20] In Mississippi, rumors of a planned slave insurrection rocked several counties in early July. The alleged massacre, to be carried out over the July Fourth holiday, was thwarted, and more than a dozen suspected ringleaders, Black and white, were hanged from the gallows. Whether the panic matched the actual threat is debatable, but the impact was not. Southern leaders railed against the abolitionist movement in increasingly strident and violent terms.

"Behold, ye 'Liberators,' 'Emancipators,' 'Abolitionists,' the fruits of your extravagance and folly, your recklessness, and your criminal plots against the lives of your fellow-men!" one southern newspaper warned.[21]

Reaction to the abolitionist mail campaign was fierce. In Charleston, South Carolina, proslavery forces wrenched open a post office window and stole sacks of newspapers to light a bonfire. An effigy of Garrison, suspended by the neck, was raised above the burning papers until it was engulfed in flames. *Library Company of Philadelphia.*

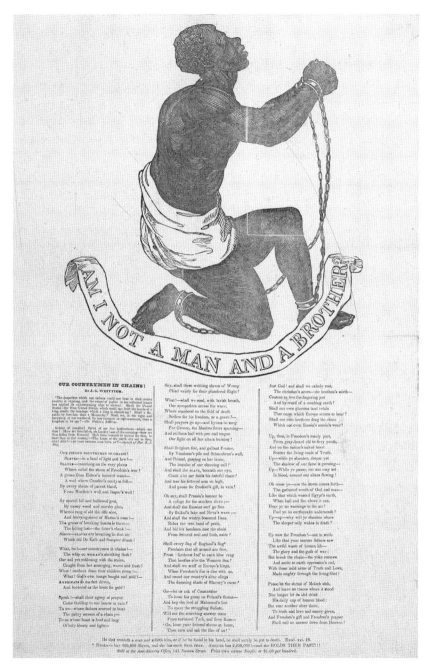

Abolitionists used this woodcut of an enslaved man with the banner "Am I not a man and a brother?" accompanied by a poem and scripture passages to help illustrate the evils of slavery. *Library of Congress.*

The southern agitation translated into northern trepidation. A deadly slave rebellion in Virginia four years earlier was still on the minds of some, and newspaper accounts did little to downplay these new fears. In Boston, the papers were filled with ominous reports of attempted slave insurrections in Mississippi, Tennessee, Kentucky and other southern states.

The abolitionists' postal campaign and its backlash fed concerns that pushing too hard on the issue of slavery would lead to violence or a civil war. To many northern whites, loyalty to the nation came before any measured distaste they might have for the institution of slavery. Some preached patience, arguing for a more gradual emancipation. Others cloaked their arguments in constitutional or states' rights terms, noting that slavery remained legal in the South. A commentator in one Boston newspaper cast the issue in particularly stark terms:

> *The Abolitionists may see in the insurrections and murders at the South the fruits of their labors, and unless the people of the non–slave holding States come out boldly, and emphatically denounce the proceeding of the headstrong bigots who are now lighting the torch of civil commotion in our land, the dissolution of the Union is as certain as that night follows day.*[22]

The Establishment Strikes Back

The issue came to a head in August 1835 as many of Boston's "most respectable" citizens called for a meeting at Faneuil Hall to reject abolitionist aims and express support for their southern brethren. Petitions were distributed around the city and quickly signed by nearly fifteen hundred leading residents, most of them merchants, artisans, shopkeepers and bankers.[23]

> *To all the friends of the Union and Constitution:*
>
> *The Citizens of Boston, without distinction of party, who are opposed to the proceedings of advocates for the immediate emancipation of the Slaves of the South—and who however they may regard slavery as an evil, yet look with distrust and abhorrence upon all measures which may tend to instigate the blacks to insubordination and insurrection,…are requested to meet at Faneuil Hall…to make known to our countrymen of the South, that we recognize their constitutional rights; that we will sustain them in*

the possession of them; and that we deplore the unauthorized interference of those, who, with a professed zeal for the melioration of the condition of the slave, are either forging for them new fetters, or placing in imminent peril the lives and property of the white population.

Mayor Lyman was not listed among the many petitioners, which is not surprising given his municipal role, but it did include his older brother, George, as well as the city's former mayor Harrison Gray Otis, who also happened to be the father-in-law of the elder Lyman. Other prominent names included Francis Cabot Lowell, Lemuel Shattuck and Amos Lawrence. Peleg Sprague, a Duxbury, Massachusetts native who had served as U.S. senator from Maine and recently resettled in Boston, also signed the petition.

The meeting was to be held on a Friday in late August in a freshly painted Faneuil Hall. It had been a clear and dry summer so far, with temperatures averaging in the high sixties—favorable weather for the vegetable markets that ran on Wednesdays at Faneuil Hall, offering cucumbers, sweet corn, beets, cabbage, melons, pears and other assorted produce. But by that Friday afternoon, the weather had turned, bringing "copious showers" with strong winds and thunder.[24]

It was an apt meteorological metaphor. That afternoon, Faneuil Hall was crowded "almost to suffocation"[25] with anti-abolitionists, and even then, some had to be turned away. After a call to order and introductory remarks, Mayor Lyman was asked to preside. He presented the issue as a constitutional matter. "We are called upon, as American citizens, to say whether we are prepared to uphold the principles of compromise from which resulted the constitution of 1789," he said.[26]

After his remarks, a series of resolutions was read by Richard Fletcher, a prominent Boston attorney. Fletcher immediately tried to frame the effort as anti-abolitionist, rather than proslavery, a system "we are bound to recognize, but are not bound to approve."[27] He claimed that since slavery existed when the nation was formed, there was no basis for northern states to question it now. But Fletcher devoted most of his remarks to a harsh critique of the abolitionists and denounced their attempts to nullify laws sustaining slavery.

"Sir, this is not reform. It is revolution," he declared.[28]

The public meeting concluded with a speech by Harrison Gray Otis, who at nearly seventy years old was one of Boston's wealthiest and best-known political leaders. Otis echoed the prior speakers and criticized the abolitionist postal campaign, mocking purported claims that the effort was designed merely to appeal to southern slaveholders' reason.

"Take a man by the throat, assail him with blows, and spit in his face—and then whisper in his ear, that you are only appealing to his reason!" he told the audience.[29]

After a full afternoon of speechmaking, the group's six resolutions were approved unanimously. Each spelled out the case against abolitionists in much the same terms as the day's speakers. All were later circulated in most of the city's newspapers.

Organizers seemed pleased with the event and the results, which they hoped would help quell the "poisonous influence" of abolitionism and calm southern fears. While it was hardly the full-throated endorsement of slavery that some southern leaders may have wanted, the resolutions did offer firm reassurances that the Boston establishment supported the status quo and valued national unity over racial equality.

Leading Boston citizens like Harrison Gray Otis feared that the abolitionists' goal of immediate emancipation of enslaved people would inflame the South and endanger the Union. *Smithsonian.*

Now, two months later, as Mayor Lyman approached the entrance of the antislavery office, he saw many of the same Boston establishment leaders collecting in the street. He read the anger on their faces and could feel the growing tension. Anti-abolitionist spirit remained high in the city, and this meeting of the Boston Female Anti-Slavery Society was quickly proving a volatile mix.

Chapter 3

MARIA CHAPMAN

When before, in this city, have gentlemen of standing and influence been incensed against a benevolent association of ladies?

Maria Weston Chapman was ready for a fight. Prior to the much-anticipated Boston Female Anti-Slavery Society meeting, she had shared her sense of apprehension with her sisters, who were also active abolitionists, but now those feelings had given way to a sense of steely resolve.

The twenty-eight-year-old Chapman did not often speak out in public—she had recently made her debut at a meeting in July—but behind the scenes, she was a growing force in the Boston abolitionist movement.[30] Initially, she helped with fundraising for antislavery causes, but her role would soon grow.

She was joined at the meeting by her husband, one of the few other men in the room. Henry Chapman, the son of a prosperous ship chandler, was already a committed abolitionist when the couple was married five years earlier, though the seeds of Maria Chapman's social activism were planted long before.[31] Her time studying in England as a teen, her experience working at a progressive school for young women and her father's early struggles with alcohol likely all contributed to her views.

Chapman grew up in a comfortable family in Weymouth, Massachusetts. Her Weston family traced its lineage back many generations to England, and some extended Weston family members had amassed great wealth, including Ezra Weston of Duxbury, Massachusetts, a shipping magnate

Above: Maria Weston Chapman, circa 1846. *BPL.*

Opposite: Chapman silhouette, circa 1830. *BPL.*

known as "King Caesar." Chapman's father, a sailor-turned-farmer, was of more modest means. She was the eldest of eight children, all of whom would eventually take roles in the antislavery cause, most notably her five sisters. Chapman was the clear leader, however, by dint of her age, ability and intellect.

Her fair appearance belied a fierce devotion to the cause of abolition. Friends described her as elegant and self-confident, "queenly in gait and manner" and always "smiling, dominant, ready to meet all comers."[32] Chapman could also come across as intense and distant. One friend praised her morals and intellect but acknowledged that her charms were not always immediately apparent. "It takes time to thaw the ice of her exterior, then you are carried away by the torrent," he recalled.[33]

Chapman and her husband now resided on West Street in Boston, a progressive enclave of the city that was home to a cluster of prominent abolitionists and friends of Garrison that came to be known as the "Boston Clique."[34] The Chapmans lived in a townhouse with their two children, three-year-old Elizabeth and Henry Jr., who was nearly one.

The Chapmans were members of the Federal Street Unitarian Church, but Maria and her sisters, who often visited, regularly attended prayer services, concerts and lectures at a variety of Boston-area churches. Earlier in the summer, they had attended an antislavery fast and traveled in a barouche, a fashionable four-wheeled carriage, "the first one by the way I was ever in," young Deborah Weston noted in her diary that day.

Enter the Foreign Agitator

For the better part of the past year, the most popular guest on the antislavery lecture circuit was not Garrison but rather the British abolitionist crusader George Thompson. Thompson had earned notoriety for a series of lectures in England and Scotland and met Garrison during his visit to London in 1833. The two men found common ground in their uncompromising abolitionist views, and Thompson made plans to make his own cross-Atlantic journey the following year.[35]

When Thompson arrived in New England, Maria Chapman and her sisters were immediately impressed. The thirty-one-year-old Liverpool native was a talented and persuasive speaker with a commanding presence and, like Garrison, preached the same immediate emancipation principles she held dear. He was "a very eloquent man," she wrote to her sister, and had "a most remarkably fine voice."

The Weston sisters were equally taken, and Maria's younger sister Deborah wrote about him frequently in her diary. Caroline Weston, who was closer in age to Maria, was also impressed with the handsome visitor. "Thompson came in, he sat an hour and was very agreeable. He read extensively from English papers which he had lately received—I am liking him better to better," she wrote.[36] On another occasion, Caroline recalled a dinner party with Thompson and his wife: "It was a horrid concern—the dinner I mean," she wrote, adding that Thompson himself was "very entertaining."[37]

Thompson visited the Chapmans' home, and his wife often socialized with Maria Chapman and her sisters. He was a welcome ally in their campaign to discredit the colonization movement—an effort to resettle free Blacks to Africa—and instead position abolitionists as the true and righteous heirs of the antislavery cause. He frequently lectured around Boston and New England, attracting supporters and detractors at nearly every stop.

The visits also proved a useful marketing tool to enlist new members and organize local antislavery chapters. A Thompson lecture in Weymouth helped spark a new group there, and in July, Maria helped organize a new chapter in nearby Hingham. Maria was often aided by her sisters, though in the case of Hingham, young Deborah "did not go to the meeting of the society as I had a bad headache," she lamented.[38]

Thompson, known to his many critics as the "foreign agitator," was also a lightning rod, and his speeches attracted plenty of controversy. Following a lecture in Abington, Massachusetts, Thompson was pelted with stones, struck in the face and met with cries of "Lynch him!"[39] He had a narrow escape from a mob in Concord, New Hampshire, and in Lynn, Massachusetts, he was greeted with rotten eggs.

The fury directed at Thompson could be attributable to a combustible mixture of ingredients, including his status as a foreigner, his talents as an orator and agitator and his strident antislavery views. Allegations that Thompson told a group of theological students that "every slave should be taught to cut his master's throat" added fuel to the fire. Thompson denied making the statement, but the words were widely reported in newspapers, and the damage was done.[40]

Garrison did not escape ire either. A few weeks after the August anti-abolitionist meeting at Faneuil Hall, a set of gallows was set up in front of his home featuring two ropes with hangman knots, presumably one each for Garrison and Thompson. Garrison responded by removing the nameplate from his front door.

Garrison's reaction to the Faneuil Hall rally, or "liberty-hating meeting," as he called it, had done little to cool tempers. He was traveling outside the state at the time, but upon his return, he lashed into the Boston establishment. "The Old Cradle has become the Coffin of Liberty!" he wrote in the *Liberator*. Garrison pointed out the hypocrisy of Otis, who had been a leader of the Hartford Convention during the War of 1812 but now preached against abolition in the name of preserving the Union.[41]

George Thompson, circa 1841. *BPL.*

Not all *Liberator* subscribers were pleased by Garrison's increasingly confrontational tone. A relative of Otis's wrote to Garrison in early September asking him to cancel his subscription to the paper, claiming that he could not support efforts "calculated to produce the terrible excitement now raging through the land."

The incidents of violence and the ratcheting up of the rhetoric were worrisome to Maria Chapman, but she remained resolute and continued with her busy schedule of abolitionist activities throughout late summer and fall. The Thompsons visited her home several days in mid-September, and she was pleased to learn that they intended to remain in the country through the winter.

She and her sisters dined with Thompson regularly and attended many of his lectures and prayer meetings. On one occasion, after another lecture before a capacity audience, the group had cake and coffee at the Weston home in Weymouth and then rode back into the city. "We had a very fine ride. Thompson telling us good stories all the way in," Deborah Weston recalled.[42]

There was growing concern for Thompson's safety each time he ventured around the New England region to preach or lecture. Chapman and her sisters had grown protective and defensive of their abolitionist ally from abroad and worried for his safety amid the attacks in the press and in the flesh. "I feel more and more assured that this man's crime was but to worship in sincerity and truth,"[43] one sister wrote.

"OH, THE VILLAINY"

In addition to celebrating her wedding anniversary in early October, Chapman was focused on her own upcoming meeting of the Boston Female Anti-Slavery Society, on whose board she now served as corresponding secretary.[44] The meeting was scheduled to be held in Congress Hall on Wednesday, October 14, the second anniversary of the society's founding.[45] Chapman and her sisters worked to spread the news in area churches that Thompson was to be the featured guest and "ladies are invited to attend."

Chapman's sister asked one friend to take the meeting notice and have it read at his church. He agreed, but she was dubious and wondered if they would really follow through.[46] The notice was read after Sunday services at the Unitarian church on Federal Street and quickly drew condemnation from the anti-abolitionist press. "It is truly surprising that Thompson should find silly women to listen to his sweeping abuse of the people of this country," the *Columbia Centinel* complained.[47]

"Has it come to this, that the *Women* of our country—not content with their proper sphere—the domestic fireside—must have public meetings to encourage a foreign emissary to destroy our peace?" wrote a correspondent in the *Boston Commercial Gazette*.[48] "Are there not sufficient deluded men already engaged in the work of abolition, that the interference of females may be dispensed with?"

Others expressed surprise that the women were moving forward with the lecture despite the rising tide of public opinion against Thompson. "We really had supposed that Thompson and his friends had experienced sufficient opposition, to prevent his persevering in attempts to disturb the peace of the community. But it would seem from the above notice that he and they are incorrigible," according to a widely circulated notice in the *Boston Centinel*.[49] They were not alone.

Two days after the church service announcement, Chapman was visited by Thompson and Garrison with bad news: the manager of Congress Hall, a Mr. J.M. Allen, had written a letter denying the women use of his building for their annual meeting. Allen made clear that his objections were not just due to the rantings of a few disgruntled residents but, rather, had come from "the most influential and respectable men in the community."[50] He even went so far as to publish the notice in the papers the next day to publicly warn that the group was forbidden from meeting, stating, "I shall take measures to exclude all persons from entering."[51]

"Oh, the villainy," thought Deborah Weston upon hearing the newspaper reaction to their planned meeting.[52] She blamed pressure from the anti-abolitionist press for causing the postponement. This was already the second location the group had chosen (the original choice, a local church, had asked for an exorbitant deposit, according to the *Liberator*, and other locations were also rejected for a variety of reasons).[53] Chapman and her sisters were clearly frustrated by all the closing doors. "Not a place can be had for love or money," one sister wrote.[54]

Many others were pleased by the development. "We hope the proprietors of every other public hall will act with the same discretion, until these foreign fomenters of disorder, shall have left the country,"[55] one Boston paper wrote.

The society issued a formal notice of the postponement and made sure to point out who they deemed responsible:

> *The Boston Female Anti Slavery Society have been informed that the proprietor and lessee of Congress Hall forbid that the annual meeting of said society should be holden at that place, under the apprehension that the building is endangered by the determination of men of* property and standing, *to put a stop to the meeting, let the consequences be what they may.*
>
> *They therefore notify the members and the public generally, that the meeting will not take place on the anniversary of the formation of the society, as was at first proposed, and as has hitherto been their practice, but will be postponed till further notice.*
>
> *By order of the Board,*
> *Mary S. Parker, Pres't.*

Chapman and a handful of other members of the Anti-Slavery Society gathered on the day their annual meeting was supposed to have taken place and decided a full board meeting was needed. That same Saturday afternoon, Chapman ventured to Ritchie Hall, where a meeting of the Ladies Moral Reform Society was being held, to share the news. There she found a rabble of men collected outside and along the staircase looking for Thompson.[56]

Mayor Lyman was called in, and the crowd of "angry and ruffian hearted men"[57] eventually dispersed without further incident.

The crowd may have gathered in the belief that the Anti-Slavery Society, rather than the Moral Reform Society, was meeting inside. It was probably not unintentional. A notice was posted on the front door of Congress Hall and nearby street corners, likely by mischief makers, claiming that Thompson would be present that afternoon. Chapman later expressed regret that the women of the Moral Reform Society had been so unceremoniously interrupted.[58]

MEETING OF THE MINDS

In response to the attempted intimidation and ongoing attacks in the press, the society decided to draft a written response. A lengthy rebuttal was penned and appeared in Saturday's edition of the *Boston Courier*. It was signed only as "A member of the Boston Female Anti-Slavery Society," though it is likely that Maria Chapman played a role in writing it.[59] The message was clear and defiant:

> *When before, in this city, have gentlemen of standing and influence been incensed against a benevolent association of ladies, for holding their annual meeting, inviting a lecturer to address them, and requesting their friends to attend…?*
>
> *This association does firmly and respectfully declare that it is our right… to hold meetings and to employ such lecturers as it judges best calculated to advance the holy cause of human rights; even though such lecturers shall chance to be foreigners.*

Chapman and her fellow board members assembled on Saturday. Following a "most excellent" prayer offered by Mary Parker,[60] they discussed plans and expressed a determination to move ahead with the annual meeting, despite the risks. The new date was set for Wednesday, October 21, at three o'clock at the antislavery office. There was no mention of Thompson in the revised notice, only that "several addresses will be delivered on the occasion."

According to Chapman's account in the society's year-end annual report, the omission was purposeful in order to protect Thompson and his family's safety, knowing he would never turn down the opportunity to speak out

THOMPSON,
THE ABOLITIONIST.

That infamous foreign scoundrel **THOMPSON**, will hold forth *this afternoon*, at the Liberator Office, No. 48, Washington Street. The present is a fair opportunity for the friends of the Union to *snake Thompson out!* It will be a contest between the Abolitionists and the friends of the Union. A purse of **$100** has been raised by a number of patriotic citizens to reward the individual who shall first lay violent hands on Thompson, so that he may be brought to the tar kettle before dark. Friends of the Union, be vigilant!

Boston, Wednesday, 12 o'clock.

In order to "wake up the populace," a group of local merchants circulated this handbill on the day of the abolitionist meeting offering a $100 bounty for Thompson. *Library of Congress.*

in support of the abolitionist cause. "We did not renew our invitation to George Thompson, for we knew that he never asks, 'what is safe?' but only, 'what is right?'"

Following the board meeting, Chapman penned a letter sharing the news and explaining the omission of Thompson's name on the revised notice, giving a somewhat different explanation. "If we could have known whether or not Mr. Thompson's engagement would permit him to come we should have stated explicitly as to that fact," she wrote.

Most of the letter was devoted to a defense of Thompson, stated with strong religious overtones. "The fact is they dread his power. What a farce—to talk of his being a foreigner! The very charge brought against the apostles whenever they taught out of their own country. What an insult to the character of God to declare themselves more just than he!" she wrote.[61]

Handbills were posted around the city with the new meeting notice, and Chapman also made some personal visits. She knew that there were significant risks associated with moving forward with their meeting—Thompson or not—and did not downplay the danger. She visited an artisan's wife who was in the middle of her sweeping duties and shared the news and the warning. The woman paused to reflect on the message. After a moment, she agreed to attend.

"I have often wished and asked that I might be able to do something for the poor slave and it seems to me that this is the very time and the very way. You shall see me at the meeting, and I will keep a prayerful mind, as I am about my work til then," the woman said.[62]

As Chapman and her colleagues prepared to finally host their annual meeting, Thompson spent time at the Garrisons' home. He continued to be subjected to withering attacks in the press. A new series of stories was circulating claiming further evidence of his alleged threat of "cutting slaveholders' throats," and new charges were raised that Thompson had committed embezzlement from a former employer in London. One newspaper claimed to have evidence in the form of signed affidavits on file for inspection at a Boston attorney's office.[63] Aside from the *Liberator* and one or two other papers, the local press was almost uniformly negative.

Chapman and her sisters were increasingly fearful for Thompson's safety and "warmly advised him not to be at the meeting."[64] Henry Chapman was also apprehensive for his wife's safety, and he and a handful of men approached Mayor Lyman, asking him to take steps to protect the women.[65]

On Tuesday evening, the night before the meeting, the Chapmans hosted dinner and were joined by Maria's sisters Anne and Deborah and other guests. The topic of abolition was raised, as expected, and no doubt there was much conversation about the looming event the following afternoon. Maria remained "very resolved" to push ahead. Henry supported her decision but continued to worry and insisted on attending the ladies' meeting in person.[66]

Wednesday brought cloudy skies and warm temperatures—and another inflammatory posting in the *Boston Commercial Gazette*. The newspaper carried a notice in block letters: "THOMPSON, THE ABOLITIONIST" and went on to share details of the women's meeting that afternoon.

"The present is a fair opportunity for the friends of the Union to snake Thompson out!" the paper wrote and offered a $100 reward to the first "patriotic citizen" to lay their hands on the abolitionist and bring him "to the tar kettle before dark."

One of the newspaper's editors, James Homer, a devoted anti-abolitionist, printed several hundred copies of a handbill with the same threatening message and had them distributed in the city's business district and among the tradesmen of the North End. His newspaper office was an unofficial headquarters for anti-abolitionist leaders in Boston. Homer later admitted that he'd been approached by two prominent local merchants with a request to write "something that would wake up the populace." Homer considered it a "business transaction" and complied "most cheerfully."[67]

One of the newspaper's young apprentices helped set the type for the handbill and recalled bringing the proof to the businessmen for approval. The men were all hanging out in a local wine room in the basement, and "there had been many drinks taken." One man had such a large wad of chewing tobacco under his lips that it distorted his face.[68]

It did not seem to matter that the newspaper and handbills were false. Thompson would not be speaking at the antislavery meeting that afternoon; he had, in fact, left the city. Chapman and her fellow board members had asked Garrison to address the society instead. But it was too late. As Garrison himself would later write, "The whole city was now wrought up to a pitch of insanity."[69]

Like Chapman, Garrison was undaunted. He expected trouble and was determined to meet it head on. After a visit from the mayor's deputy in the morning, he reluctantly, and somewhat resentfully, offered his assurances that Thompson was not around. He then returned to his home for an early meal with a friend from out of town, John B. Vashon, a successful Black merchant who helped support the *Liberator* financially.

Before returning to the antislavery office that afternoon to meet with Maria Chapman, Susan Paul and their fellow society members, Garrison posted a letter with a friend that he had penned earlier that morning. His words would prove prophetic:

> *Nevertheless, let the worst appear; let not our sin be covered up; let the number of the rebels, and the extent of the rebellion, fully appear; let all that is dangerous, or hypocritical, or unjust among us be proclaimed upon the house-tops; and then the genuine disciples of Christ will be able skillfully and understandingly to carry on the war.*[70]

Chapter 4

WENDELL PHILLIPS

The proud leader of the aristocracy.

Wendell Phillips was working in his office on Court Street when he first heard the yelling and shouting. The young attorney looked out his window to see what was causing the disturbance and saw a crowd parading in the streets. Whatever was happening had to be more interesting than the contracts, wills and workaday woes that normally composed his nascent law practice. Phillips put down his books and ventured outside "to see what the excitement was."[71]

He noticed some women, a few children, but mostly men gathering outside in the streets near the Old State House. Many of the men wore fashionable English and French broadcloth coats like his own. They were merchants, shopkeepers, tradesman, bankers and militia members. They looked angry. And they looked like him.

Wendell Phillips was, by all accounts, a gentleman of property and standing. The young lawyer had recently opened his practice in Boston after graduating from the Boston Latin School, Harvard College and Harvard Law School. He hailed from an Old Boston family; was the son of Boston's first mayor, John Phillips; and had enjoyed an aristocratic upbringing in an expansive Beacon Hill home.

Phillips had been blessed in many ways. Friends described him as strikingly handsome, refined and charming. He was tall and athletic, with a muscular physique, and skilled at boxing, fencing and horsemanship.

"Handsome, indeed, in form and features," recalled one classmate.[72] He was a leading member of the most exclusive social clubs, a devout Bible reader and known for his plain-spoken eloquence.

His oratorical skills were equally lauded. As a young man, Phillips was invited to give a Fourth of July speech in the fishing port of New Bedford. He spoke about the state's political history, and his rhetorical talents were apparent.[73] "When he stood up in the pulpit I thought him the handsomest man I had ever seen; when he began to speak, his elocution seemed the most beautiful to which I had ever listened," a local journalist recalled many years later.

Wendell Phillips, circa 1841. *BPL.*

Phillips was an above-average student, interested in history and mathematics. He was a quick learner, though not a natural academic—one who "sauntered and gently studied."[74] He pursued his law degree but did not appear to have any special fondness for the law.[75]

While known for his faith and decency, Phillips was certainly no reformer. In fact, he helped defeat efforts to establish the first temperance society at Harvard. Any efforts he might have undertaken to offer aid to the poor and other marginalized members of society came more from a grand sense of morality, rather than any belief in radical social change. He was, in short, "the proud leader of the aristocracy," as his alma mater once described him.

"In a good sense of the words, he was a born patrician; in the sense of the French expression 'noblesse oblige,'" a Harvard classmate recalled. "He felt the responsibilities of his birth and education,—his responsibility to keep himself pure, upright, and good."[76]

After a brief stint practicing law in Lowell as an apprentice, Phillips returned to Boston in 1835 and opened his own practice. He rented space in the same building as another scion of a famed Boston family, John C. Winthrop, who was already making a name for himself in state politics. He socialized with many of the up-and-coming young lawyers who had offices nearby, including a former schoolmate named Charles Sumner.

Phillips joined the local militia regiment, as many young men of his age did. He also developed an interest in his own family history and remained a "voracious reader" of ancient and modern literature, no doubt frequenting

Burdett's foreign bookshop located across from his office.[77] There were few hints that Phillips would do anything other than continue along his expected trajectory toward further success, wealth and prestige.

RINGLEADERS OF THE RABBLE

Phillips pushed his way through the unruly crowd. Ahead was the Old State House, and to his left a short distance was the antislavery office on Washington Street. There were already hundreds of men in the streets, and it was quickly transforming from crowd to mob. The incendiary handbills distributed around the city were having their desired impact.

A couple of blocks east on Chatham Street, a young printer's apprentice had delivered the handbill to a local oil and candle shop. The city's first gas streetlights had been introduced a few years earlier, but oil lamps were still the main source of illumination for most Boston residents, and whale oil was a valued commodity. Upon reading the notice, the shopkeeper called out for "a bucket of green tar" so they could be ready to tar and feather the abolitionist.[78]

Phillips did not feel the same urgency. There is no record that he attended the anti-abolitionist rally at Faneuil Hall in August, nor did he express any support or enthusiasm for the abolitionist cause or the plight of enslaved people. Though educated and read, he was not well-traveled and only rarely ventured outside his comfortable conservative bubble. "I did not understand anti-slavery then," he later admitted.[79]

The ringleaders of the rabble were men who—if Phillips did not know them personally—certainly drew from similar social and political spheres. Isaac Means was a merchant and ward leader who served on the board of directors for a local bank. Isaac Stevens was a partner at Stevens, Fisher and Co. on Central Wharf and served on the board of an insurance company and a bank. Means and Stevens both played a key role in having the Thompson handbill printed and circulated, as did Henry Williams, another banker and Central Wharf merchant, described as red faced with white hair.

Another prominent ringleader was a man named John L. Dimmock, a Central Wharf merchant who served as president at South Bank. He was a Whig and a political supporter of Lyman and Daniel Webster. Dimmock and Williams were among a select committee of men who reviewed the Thompson handbill on Wednesday morning before it was distributed.

Phillips's law office was located near the Old State House, just a short distance from the antislavery office where the women's meeting was being held. *BPL.*

Although the leaders were united in their hostility toward abolitionists, they did not all agree on tactics. Some, like Dimmock, had reservations about the handbill, while others were eager to go on the offensive. Williams, in his "usually loud and boisterous way," said he looked forward to giving Thompson and Garrison a "good coat of tar and feathers."[80]

Dimmock also served as state representative from Boston, and he and his colleagues in the legislature had an afternoon session scheduled at the State House. Word was spreading fast that "a multitude assembled were going to mob Garrison…and also one Thompson,"[81] so rather than take their seats for the two o'clock session, some legislators decided to head down to check it out—some, like Phillips, as spectators, and others likely as more active participants.

State Representative Ellis Ames from the small town of West Bridgewater was among the former. After hearing the news, he left the State House chamber and walked down Beacon Hill toward the antislavery office. His path took him along Court Street, where he passed by Wendell Phillips's law office.

As he moved through the crowd, Ames picked up bits and pieces of conversations. The prevailing sentiment seemed to be that southerners would not trade with Boston merchants if newspapers such as the *Liberator* were allowed to malign them, he recalled.

"I remember that several men stood debating, and one of them said that this…was the only way to stop Garrison's paper; that, under our Constitutions, a libelous paper could not be stopped in advance," Ames recounted later. Government "muzzling" of the press had stopped wars in Europe, the man argued, and since that was not an option here, mob action was necessary. If papers such as the *Liberator* were not suppressed, "war would ensue between the North and South," Ames recollected.[82]

Ames found a safe vantage, probably not far from Phillips, and watched as Mayor Lyman arrived on the scene. The mayor stepped into the entryway of the antislavery office and ascended a few steps to gain a better view of the crowd in the street. What he saw was concerning. "The mob was becoming more boisterous and inflamed," Lyman saw. "I was well satisfied we were menaced with a serious riot."

Phillips was observing the mayor too and shared the same concerns about escalating tempers. He listened as the mayor now attempted to quiet the restless crowd. Apart from his walking cane and handful of deputies, Lyman had few resources at his disposal.

At one point, a figure emerged from the front of the antislavery office, and the crowd mistakenly assumed he was Thompson. They rushed forward and seized the unfortunate man. "We could see the poor devil thumped and kicked and otherwise roughly used," one witness said later.[83] Henry Williams soon jumped into the fray and in his deep baritone voice yelled, "Kill him, kill him!"

If the scene now playing out before the antislavery society meeting disturbed Phillips, he did not articulate it at the time. Boston's gentlemen of property and standing had been awakened, and these "mobocrats in broadcloth" would not be going quietly.

The remaining question now was which side Phillips was on.

Chapter 5

THE MEETING

Is Mr. Thompson here in petticoats?

Inside the building on the third floor, Maria Chapman, Susan Paul and the women of the Boston Female Anti-Slavery Society prepared to finally start their anticipated meeting. The women were arrayed on benches toward the front of the lecture hall. Chapman's husband was in attendance along with one other man, but otherwise, the only men in the hall were the unwelcome visitors glaring from over the partition at the rear of the room.

A short time before three o'clock, there were murmurs in the crowd as Garrison arrived and climbed the two flights past the "noisy intruders" to enter the hall. "That's Garrison! That's Garrison!" came the rowdy chorus of voices.

He was accompanied by a friend, Charles Burleigh. They made for an unlikely-looking pair: Burleigh, with his long sandy hair and full flowing beard, was known for his colorful personality, standing in contrast to the serious-minded, pious and nearly bald-pated Garrison. But the men shared a devotion to the cause of abolition; Burleigh published an antislavery newspaper in Connecticut, lectured frequently and contributed to the *Liberator*.[84]

Garrison and Burleigh pushed through the crowd and took their seats inside the hall. Garrison's wife, Helen, was less fortunate. She arrived late and found the outside entrance blocked by the throngs of protestors. Despite being several months pregnant, she wanted to attend to support

Left: Charles Burleigh. *BPL*. *Right*: Helen Garrison. *LOC*.

the women of the Anti-Slavery Society and make the point that "though there might be many to molest, there were none that could make afraid," her husband recounted.[85]

Helen Garrison was hardly alone in her predicament. Chapman reported that as many as one hundred women were prevented from entering the hall.[86] One of them was fifteen-year-old Sarah Southwick, who was disappointed to learn that she and her sister had arrived too late. Her mother, Thankful Southwick, had left earlier and was already inside.[87]

Caroline Weston, Chapman's sister, was also stymied. When she first arrived, the path to the door appeared clear, but then "the sudden rush of the mob of all assorts of people from every street and avenue in sight was so sudden and overpowering that with the greatest difficulty I made my way to the foot of the staircase and never succeeded in mounting."[88]

Some of the women who did successfully navigate the gauntlet were greeted with catcalls and insults. "One or two of the colored ladies were rudely pushed into the hall," Burleigh recalled.[89]

Garrison may have been hoping that his presence—rather than the more detested Thompson—would persuade the uninvited guests in the entryway to depart so the meeting could take place uninterrupted. When it became clear that it would not, he rose and turned to address them.

"Gentlemen, perhaps you are not aware that this is a meeting of the Boston Female Anti-Slavery Society, called and intended exclusively for ladies, and those only who have been invited to address them. Understanding this fact, you will not be so rude or indecorous as to thrust your presence upon this meeting," Garrison stated.

"If, gentlemen, any of you are ladies—in disguise—why, only apprise me of the fact, give me your names, and I will introduce you to the rest of your sex, and you can take seats among them accordingly," he needled.[90]

His words briefly quieted the crowd, but the peace was momentary, and the men soon grew more brazen and boisterous. Garrison did not expect a friendly reception, but he now realized he had underestimated the level of hostility. "I went, not knowing indeed what things would befall me, but having no doubt that the malignity of the crowd would be transferred from Mr. Thompson to myself," he explained later.

The women called for the door to the hall to be shut so the meeting could begin, Chapman recalled, but the men "could not decide as to whether the request should be granted, and the door was opened and shut with violence, till it hung useless from the upper hinge."[91]

Chapman could see that Garrison's continued presence was proving a disruption and would likely prevent the women from being able to proceed. Garrison concurred. He rose to converse with Mary Parker and offered to leave.

"It was her earnest wish that I would retire, as well for my own safety as for the peace of the meeting," Garrison said. "She assured me that the Society would resolutely but calmly proceed to the transaction of its business and leave the issue with God."[92]

Rather than venturing back downstairs via the stairwell, which was jammed with angry men, Garrison crossed through the landing area and wisely decided to take shelter in the adjacent office on the other side of the partition. He was joined by his friend Burleigh.

"It was deemed prudent to lock the door, to prevent the mob from rushing in and destroying our publications," Garrison explained. He promptly sat down at his work desk, which faced out through a window onto Washington Street, and began composing a letter to a friend about the day's events.

Maria Chapman and her fellow members could not see through the crowded entryway and assumed that Garrison had made it down the stairs and back out to the street. They decided to move ahead with the meeting. When the clock struck three o'clock, Mary Parker called the group to order. Her voice was "clear and firm."[93]

The hecklers in the rear remained mistrustful. "Is Mr. Thompson here in petticoats?" one man called out. Chapman recognized the man and later noted—without ever revealing his name—that he was a "well known" person.[94]

The women ignored the shouts and knelt for an opening prayer and scripture reading. They were interrupted at one point by a flying board, five or six feet in length, which was tossed into the room from the other side of the partition. It landed harmlessly. Some of the men pushed forward on the partition and succeeded in partially breaking it on one side.

Inside the room, Garrison could hear the women's solemn prayers over the hisses, threats and curses. He drew inspiration from their words in the face of the hostile men. "It was an awful, sublime and soul-thrilling scene— enough, one would suppose, to melt adamantine hearts, and make even fiends of darkness stagger and retreat," he recalled.

The crowd pressed forward against the door to Garrison's office. They succeeded in kicking in one of the lower panels and spotted the editor sitting at a desk. "There he is! That's Garrison! Out with the scoundrel!" they cried out.

Garrison was resigned to his fate and told Burleigh to go ahead and open the full door. "Let them come in and do their worst," he said. But his friend had other ideas. He stepped out into the hall and locked the door behind him from the outside, securing the key in his pocket. Burleigh then stood guard by the door in a "calm and firm demeanor," determined to protect Garrison. He succeeded—for the moment—and the men stood down.

From their vantage, neither Maria Chapman nor Susan Paul nor any of the other women of the Boston Female Anti-Slavery Society may have known of Garrison's close call, but they all certainly understood how volatile the situation had become. And it was about to be complicated by the arrival of another visitor.

Chapter 6

LAST BULWARK

Ladies, do you wish to see a scene of bloodshed, and confusion?
If you do not, go home.

Mayor Lyman could see that events were fast escalating out of his control. His calculation that Thompson's absence would diffuse the situation had proven incorrect. Whether the target was Thompson, Garrison or the ladies of the Boston Female Anti-Slavery Society seemed to be irrelevant; anyone who wore the mantel of abolitionist was in danger.

Lyman pushed his way upstairs and found the women seated in the lecture hall starting their meeting. Most had their backs to him as he entered. The society's recording secretary, Martha V. Ball, who taught night classes for young Black women at Susan Paul's church, had just risen to read her report.

The mayor was surprised to see the large number of men clogging the landing and entryway to the lecture hall. There were about twenty or thirty crowded by the door, half of whom he described as "lads." The dense throng made it difficult to get in or out.

The mayor's primary concern was for the safety of the women. He did not believe the mob presented any physical threat to them but still worried what might happen and wanted to avoid more hostilities. He knew the presence of several Black women, including Susan Paul, mixed in the audience would surely antagonize the already intolerant crowd outside.

"Go home, ladies, go home," the mayor counseled.

"What renders it necessary we should go home?" asked Mary Parker. The conversation was later relayed in detail by Maria Chapman, though Mayor Lyman recalled the exchange somewhat differently.[95]

"I am the mayor of the city, and I cannot now explain; but will call upon you this evening," Lyman said.

Parker responded, "If the ladies will be seated, we will take the sense of the meeting."

"Don't stop, ladies, go home," Lyman replied.

At this point, Parker shared an offer from Francis Jackson, a prominent local abolitionist, who had volunteered the use of his home to the women for their meetings.

Lyman again urged them to dissolve the meeting and disperse. "Ladies, do you wish to see a scene of bloodshed and confusion? If you do not, go home."

Chapman found the mayor's words cowardly and insulting. She placed much of the blame for the anti-abolitionist hostilities on the mayor's own political supporters, whom he now professed to be powerless to stop. He was supposed to be the mayor of the city, yet here he was "pale with terror, ordering us out of our own hall at the command of a mob."[96] Some of the women may not have wished to challenge Lyman, but Chapman had no such reluctance. She turned and addressed him directly:

"Mr. Lyman, your personal friends are the instigators of this mob; have you ever used your personal influence with them?" she asked pointedly.

"I know no personal friends; I am merely an official," Lyman said. "Indeed, ladies, you must retire. It is dangerous to remain."

"If this is the last bulwark of freedom, we may as well die here, as anywhere," Chapman replied, in words that would later become an abolitionist rallying cry.[97]

Lyman smiled. He replied that he did not believe the women's lives were in danger but repeated his advice that it was time to end the meeting. "Do you wish to prolong this scene of confusion?" he asked. Apart from Maria Chapman, who seemed to aspire to martyrdom, he thought the women appeared ready to leave.

Parker asked the mayor if the women could pass out safely.

"If you will go now, I will protect you, but cannot unless you do," Lyman said.

The women agreed, and a motion was made and approved to adjourn the meeting. Lyman led the way down, pushing back the crowd to create an egress amid groans, hissing and laughter. One witness described the procession as a "long lane of ruffians dressed in broadcloth."[98]

Chapman remained resentful that the Anti-Slavery Society's duly commenced meeting could be interrupted in this shameful manner—and by men who were supposed to be *gentlemen*. She helped lead the women down the flights of stairs; the passageway was darkened by the men blocking the windows, but she could see well enough.

"We could identify those faces, even if we had never seen them before," she said.

By the time the women exited the building, it was nearing four o'clock in the afternoon, and clouds were overhead. When they emerged into the daylight, a "roar of rage and contempt" came from the crowd assembled on the street.

Chapman remained resolute and did not want to give in to this gentlemen's mob. She arranged for the women to march in a procession, walking next to their Black members to offer a measure of protection and no doubt a show of defiance.

"Two and two, to Francis Jackson's, Hollis Street, each with a colored friend," she counseled.

The sight of the women boldly marching in pairs, Black and white, arm in arm, drew hisses from men in the crowd. An account in one anti-abolitionist newspaper called the women "as silly as can be imagined."[99]

The crowd continued their jeering but parted sufficiently to permit the procession to advance. The original twenty-five or so women who were upstairs for the meeting swelled in number as others like Sarah Southwick and Caroline Weston, who had been prevented from getting inside, now joined them.

As Chapman marched south on Washington Street with her colleagues, she looked outward and was disgusted by what she saw. There were hundreds and hundreds of men arrayed on both sides of the street. These were the wealthy and respectable of Boston, men of "influence and standing." *How did they not know better?* she thought.

"We saw the faces of those we had, till now, thought friends;— men whom we never before met without giving the hand in friendly salutation;—men whom till now we should have called upon for condemnation of ruffianism, with confidence that the appeal would be answered," she said.

As much as she and her allies detested those southern gentlemen who defended and perpetuated slavery, these men were in some ways worse. They knew better. They denounce "slavery in the abstract" and "thank God that New England is free from the curse," she thought, and yet today here they threaten "murderous outrages" against those abolitionists who seek merely to match action to those same beliefs.

"In conversing with persons from the South, we have found more openness, more candor, more toleration even, than in Northern opposers," she said.

The women originally headed for the home of Francis Jackson but soon learned that his wife was ill, so they changed course and headed to Chapman's home on West Street to complete the business of their meeting.

If Chapman felt any temporary sense of relief at having avoided the worst of the mob, it was soon replaced with a sense of dread as she learned that Garrison had not escaped, as she had assumed, but rather was still trapped inside the building. She now regretted her decision to listen to the mayor and leave the office.

"This was an unexpected blow," she admitted.

Chapter 7

SIGN OF THE TIMES

The faces of these wretches while making these assaults seemed transformed with malice and passion. I never recollect seeing such a diabolical exhibition.

Mayor Lyman was growing concerned. He was not having much luck controlling the mob, which had now swelled to over one thousand men. Neither the absence of Thompson nor the departure of the female abolitionists had quieted them. He had only a handful of peace officers on hand to assist, and soon the sun would be setting.

"We had the prospect before us of a most stormy night," he said.

Lyman feared for the potential loss of life and property damage that might occur at the hands of an unchecked mob. The merchants who rented space on the first floor of the antislavery building had already sounded the alarm, fearful for the safety of their shops and goods and angered by the ongoing presence of the abolitionists.

Lyman stood up on a chair on the street and tried to address the crowd, warning them to disperse and return to their homes. He reminded them that, contrary to the notorious handbill circulating, Thompson was not even believed to be in the city. His words were likely a futile gesture, and the vigor of his protestations was later debated.

Representative Ellis Ames, venturing over from the State House, watched the scene and later criticized the mayor for not speaking out forcefully enough. "I well remember that [he] was very small around his chest and across his breast, and it then seemed to me that it was impossible for him to speak louder than he did."[100]

Others disputed Ames's account. "[Mayor Lyman's] voice was decidedly strong," said one witness, noting that Lyman was nearly six feet tall, "well-proportioned and active."[101]

Whichever account came closer to the truth would not matter. The mob had awoken and would not be easily dissuaded. At first, the crowd did not seem to believe the mayor's assurances that Thompson was not present, but they soon retrained their fire. A conversation between two southern gentlemen in the crowd exemplified the dire stakes now facing the mayor. The exchange was overheard and later relayed in the newspaper.

"The mayor says Thompson is not in the city but…I don't believe him," one gentleman was heard to say.

"Well! Garrison is here if Thompson isn't. They are after Garrison now," the second gentleman replied.

"I hope they will catch him. I would give five thousand dollars for him," said the first.

"Yes! If we could get him on board your packet [ship to the South] we would take care of him," the other man replied.[102]

The cries for Garrison continued to circulate. He remained upstairs in the office, though there was some disagreement as to his precise whereabouts at the time. At one point, a handful of men rushed forward from the street and charged for the door to pursue Garrison, but they were blocked by the mayor's constables, Derastus Clapp and Nathaniel Coolidge.

Some of the men who were already upstairs when the ladies left the hall began to hurl books out the window onto the street below. They may have assumed the books were antislavery propaganda, but they were actually prayer books left behind by an Episcopal church group that used the antislavery hall on Sundays.[103] A voice in the crowd sarcastically called out for some abolitionist tracts, to which one of the mayor's deputies cheerfully replied, "We have no tracts for distribution."[104]

One abolitionist who had the misfortune to exit the hall at the wrong time was David Ela, editor of *Zion's Herald*, a progressive religious newspaper. Ela was mistaken for Garrison and pummeled with ten or twelve blows, though he escaped serious injury.[105] He may have been accompanied by John T. Hilton, a local barber, merchant and prominent Black abolitionist who was an officer in the Massachusetts Anti-Slavery Society. Hilton's wife, Lavinia, was among the female members who had just left the building.

The increasing violence and vitriol of the crowd were alarming to some witnesses. "The faces of these wretches while making these assaults seemed transformed with malice and passion. I never recollect seeing such a diabolical exhibition," one abolitionist later recalled.[106]

Wendell Phillips also watched the scene as the mayor tried to manage the crowd and had a different question; something did not make sense to him. He spotted a fellow attorney named John C. Park whose law office was across the street from his. Park was president of the Irish Society and served as a colonel in his local militia regiment.

"Why does not the mayor call out the regiment?" Phillips asked. "We would cheerfully take arms in such a case as this. It is a very shameful business. Why does he stand there arguing? Why does he not call for the guns?"

Park gestured to the crowd, advising his colleague that the mob and the militia were one and the same. Phillips later acknowledged his own naivete: "I did not know that the guns were in the street—that the men who should have borne them were the mob; that all there was of government in Boston was in the street," he said.

It was a chilling realization for Phillips, and the memory would stick with him long after that day. This was not how gentlemen of property and standing were expected to act. Phillips certainly didn't consider himself an abolitionist and probably shared many of the same apathetic views of the antislavery cause as other men his age. He was standing here in the streets, however, and thus was at least tacitly part of the mob, though he considered himself only a spectator.

The crowd's attention soon turned to a large wooden sign that read "Anti-Slavery Rooms."[107] The sign ran lengthwise along the front of the building and was at least six feet in length. "Tear down the sign!" came the cries from the crowd.[108]

The clamor caught the ear of Mayor Lyman. With Garrison out of eyesight, Thompson absent and the female abolitionists now departed, the antislavery sign became the mob's next target. "I suppose it was the only thing they could see that reminded them of the object of their vengeance," he explained.[109]

Lyman feared that, as it now began to get dark, the mob would start launching rocks at the sign. The city had just finished resurfacing State Street, and there were plenty of spare stones about that could be used as projectiles. If the crowd started pelting the sign, they could easily end up breaking windows in the building, he thought, and the landlord was already cross about having his property damaged. The mayor also worried that his own constables might get injured in the process and then things could escalate quickly.

This sarcastic cartoon depicting the scene outside the antislavery office shows the anti-abolitionists dressed in top hats, attacking the sign and throwing Bibles out the window. "Down with the damned Abolitionists! The peace of the city is destroyed. Lynch them! Lynch them!" it read in a mocking tone. Two men toasting prominent anti-abolitionists are shown in shabby clothes, one with a wine bottle in hand. "Our liberties must be preserved. Lynch the rascals!" one said. Another man is seen stepping on a sheet of paper labeled "human rights." The provenance of the cartoon is unknown, but it may have been drawn contemporaneously. *BPL.*

John Dimmock, one of the anti-abolitionist leaders, agreed. "You had better take in that sign," he advised, making it clear that if no one else did, he was prepared to take action.[110] Lyman hesitated at first—one witness described him as "exceedingly agitated"—and then reluctantly agreed it was best to head off any problem, so he sent a deputy to see if the sign could be removed.

Henry Williams and one or two of the mayor's men climbed the stairs to the third floor and opened the windows. Using a hammer, they loosened the fastenings holding up the sign, took it off the hooks and lowered it to the pavement below. The mayor said later that he asked the men to remove the sign and store it inside the lecture room, rather than lower it to the ground, but that request was apparently ignored.

Predictably, the sign was vandalized as soon as it fell to the ground and banged against a nearby lamppost. Souvenir hunters rushed forward to snatch up broken bits of the "wicked Abolition board," which they passed among the crowd.

"I procured a piece about three inches wide, and some six feet long, as a trophy of the battle," one witness boasted later. He brought it to the *Boston Commercial Gazette* office, where the publisher chopped it in smaller pieces to hand out to anti-abolitionists as mementos. One piece was cut into a coffin shape and sent out of state.[111] Another witness recalled overhearing a man who got a splinter saying he would "send it for a toothpick to a slaveholder" he knew.[112]

Not every souvenir seeker was hostile. One *Liberator* supporter named Hiram Blanchard took a piece of the sign as a keepsake. He remained a devoted subscriber and kept the sign splinter in his home for many years until it was eventually lost.[113]

The mayor's exact role in the removal of the sign was later disputed. The symbolism of the sign's removal struck a nerve with abolitionists, who accused the mayor of purposefully ordering its destruction in an act of appeasement.

"The value of the article destroyed was of no consequence," said Garrison, "but the principal involved in its surrender and sacrifice is one upon which civil government, private property and individual liberty depend."[114]

For his part, Mayor Lyman maintained that he merely "sanctioned" the sign's removal and that his motivation was rooted in pacifying the crowd to avoid further violence, rather than any animosity toward the abolitionists. He later criticized Garrison and others who perpetuated what he felt was a false narrative regarding the sign removal.

The destruction of the antislavery sign seemed to satisfy—or at least distract—the mob for the time being, and there was a lull in the hostilities. But if anyone thought the worst was over, they would soon learn otherwise.

Chapter 8

GREAT ESCAPE

Catch them! Hang him! Death to the damned abolitionist!

Garrison remained upstairs in the antislavery office, essentially trapped. The crowd outside, now estimated at several thousand by some witness accounts, made it nearly impossible for him to exit safely through the front door. With darkness coming, there was a renewed push to get him out of the building before the mob decided to adopt even more aggressive tactics.

Charles Burleigh remained at Garrison's side and noted that despite all the tumult, he remained "calm, collected and cheerful."[115] He nonetheless feared for his friend's safety and counseled that it was time to make his escape. On this point, Mayor Lyman agreed, as the cries for "Garrison!" among the crowd had resumed and grown in intensity.

"Can't you go up in the attic and hide yourself?" Lyman reportedly asked.[116] He was anxious to get Garrison out of the building, or at least concealed, and did not believe he could be protected much longer. After a brief conversation, Lyman climbed down the stairs and returned to the front entrance of the building. His deputy sheriff called down to the crowd.

Some of Garrison's supporters wondered if it would be better to take a stand and defend their rights since the civil authority seemed incapable of doing so. *Might it be time to repudiate his cherished principle of nonresistance?* one friend asked.

Garrison was reluctant to leave the building, but he would not entertain the thought of any active resistance. He put a hand on a friend's shoulder. "I will perish sooner than raise my hand against any man, even in self-defense and let none of my friends resort to violence for my protection," he said.[117]

Garrison's friend John Campbell had managed to sneak past the mob into the antislavery office and now suggested that they escape via a window facing the back of the building. Campbell was a fellow officer of the New England Anti-Slavery Society, and he had traveled with Garrison and Thompson to New York and Philadelphia in March to spread the abolitionist message.

This next excursion would be a different kind of trip. Campbell knew there was a carpenter's shop nearby that might offer sanctuary since the owner, Luke Brown, was known to be friendly to the antislavery cause. With Campbell leading the way and acting as a bodyguard, he and Garrison climbed out of the rear window, which was about twenty-five feet above ground, and then dropped onto an adjacent shed.

As he made his exit, Garrison was reported to have theatrically exclaimed, "Hail Columbia, happy land," the first words of a patriotic song known as the "President's March," which was then the de facto national anthem. If he did speak the words, it was certainly done in a mocking tone, though it may have just been an embellishment of the anti-abolitionist press.

A small number of supporters followed out of the building, though Garrison himself almost didn't make it. As he dropped from the back window, a small box he was standing on gave way, and he "narrowly escaped falling headlong to the ground," he recalled.[118]

The men made the short dash toward the shop, which abutted a narrow street called Wilson's Lane. "Luke Brown's carpenter shop—to Brown's shop!" was their rallying cry.[119]

They were not alone.

The carpenter's abolitionist sympathies were well known, and some of the rioters anticipated that Garrison might try to flee there. A crowd of as many as two hundred men gathered in the rear of building and now blocked off access to the main street. The rioters spotted Garrison and gave chase. "Catch them! Hang him! Death to the damned abolitionist!" the men yelled out in pursuit.[120]

One of them was a young man named Josiah Fuller, who worked at a fashionable barbershop on nearby Congress Street. The shop owner was originally from Sicily, and his clientele included many of Boston's leading citizens, including Daniel Webster, the U.S. senator and now a Whig candidate for president.[121]

Fuller, just eighteen years old, had given Webster a shave on several occasions, and the senator's anti-abolitionist views had rubbed off. "My head was filled with pro-slavery sentiment derived from Webster's eloquent words," he admitted.[122]

After lunch, Fuller mixed in with the mob in front of the antislavery office, probably not far from Wendell Phillips. He followed the crowds after hearing someone shout, "Let us go around to Wilson's Lane."

While Fuller and the other men gave chase, Garrison and his handful of supporters split up. He and Campbell rushed toward the carpenter's shop, while others tried to divert attention in other directions. Luke Brown had left his shop for the day already, but several of his apprentices were still at work, and when they spotted Garrison, they realized what was happening and sprang into action. Once Garrison was safely inside, the apprentices swung the shop door closed to keep the mob at bay for the time being.

Once he had a moment to catch his breath and reflect, Garrison felt the futility of his situation. He told his friend that he thought it might be better to surrender to the mob "and let them deal with me as they might elect." Campbell disagreed and advised his friend to do everything he could to stay out of their clutches.

Garrison climbed to the loft on the second floor of the shop, and one of the workers hid him under a pile of lumber and wood chips in the corner. Another "stalwart" apprentice stood by the front entrance waving a broadax to ward off the mob.

"I'll split the skull of the first man who attempts to come in," the brawny young apprentice warned. He was vastly outnumbered by the mob but nonetheless cast an intimidating presence. "Stand back! Stand back!" he repeated.[123]

The standoff continued for a few tense minutes. Eventually, it was agreed that a delegation of three or four young men would be permitted to enter the carpenter's shop and conduct a search. It was a calculated risk. Garrison was well hidden, and it was hoped he might elude detection so that the mob would assume he'd fled and carry on their search elsewhere.

The mob contingent entered and began an exhaustive search of the shop, including the basement and loft. They soon spotted Campbell, who was pretending to be an apprentice laboring at work. His ruse did not succeed. Under pointed questioning Campbell's real identity was quickly deduced, and the men grabbed him and dragged him outside in front of the crowd.

"This is not Garrison, but Garrison's friend, and he says he knows where Garrison is but, won't tell," one of the ringleaders shouted out.

What happened next is unclear. Campbell may have revealed Garrison's location under pressure, or the mob may have discovered it on their own. There were more shouts from the crowd, and Campbell managed to break away, but the end result was that Garrison's hiding spot in the loft was discovered.

The rioters seized Garrison, shook him roughly to shake off the wood chips and pushed him over to the loft door, which was now open and letting in light. In the tussle, he lost his coat and hat. While the mob watched from below, several young men held Garrison and threatened to toss him to the pavement.

One of them was a stout young man named Benjamin Willis, who was known to be a troublemaker. He was roommates with one of the newspaper apprentices at the *Boston Commercial Gazette* who had helped distribute the Thompson handbill earlier in the day.[124] Willis grabbed a nearby rope used by the carpenters for hanging windows and tied it around Garrison's waist under his arms.

"Throw him out of the door!" came the cry from the crowd.

"Let's not kill him *that way*," said another.

"Don't hurt him!" a friendlier voice from the crowd spoke out. "He ain't English."[125]

The plea was heeded, probably because the young men had more nefarious plans in store for Garrison, and instead a plank or ladder was raised and angled against the side of the building. Willis lowered an upright Garrison to the ground as he faced the hostile crowd.

Garrison's reaction to being discovered was also disputed. An account in the anti-abolitionist press later claimed that a frightened Garrison fell onto his knees and prayed for mercy, "and when assured that no one should hurt him, he seemed scarcely to know what was said to him, or what he was about."[126]

"This is altogether false," Garrison countered. "It is needless to make such extra efforts of violence—I shall go down to the mob unresistingly," he recalled telling his captors.

Whether he showed it or not, Garrison had cause for worry. A group of men, which probably included Willis, had assembled before the women's antislavery meeting to plot and make preparations against the abolitionists. They gathered supplies, including a stock of tar, feathers, corrosive liquor and indelible ink.[127]

A young boy who didn't have school that afternoon heard the excitement and followed the rioters as they pursued Garrison. He had vivid recollections many years later: "I was one of the youngsters who ran with the crowd....I was too late to see the ejectment from the shop but mounted the regular stairs and gained the roof of the building. Looking over the edge into the lane, there was Garrison bareheaded, his baldness visible from my perch, with a rope about his body, and he both dragged and pushed the throng about him. Occasionally a rioter would make a sudden dash at him to strike him or tear," the boy recalled.[128]

The men intended to drag Garrison (and, they had hoped, Thompson) to the Boston Common, where they would tar and feather their target, dunk him in the Frog Pond and then dye his hands and face black with the ink "in a manner that would never change from a night negro color."[129]

Thompson may have escaped, but Garrison was not so lucky.

Chapter 9

TRUCKMAN TO THE RESCUE

To the Frog Pond with him!

Mayor Lyman was still stationed on Washington Street in front of the antislavery office and did not witness Garrison's departure. With the help of his constables, he'd been trying to hold off the mob and prevent a full-scale assault on the building. When he heard that the abolitionists had escaped out the back window, he breathed a sigh of relief. "I thought the danger of a boisterous night was now much diminished," he said.

A spectator soon broke the bad news: Garrison had been caught. At first, Lyman did not believe the report; he had just escaped the building, how was he caught so fast? The spectator filled him in on the details, and the news sank in. Further confirmation came from the crowd itself, which was now scrambling toward the Old State House, a short distance away.

Garrison's friend Charles Burleigh also saw the crowd thinning rapidly and at first thought it was good news. He assumed that many of the gentlemen had given up and were returning to their homes, "but it was not long before I discovered my mistake."[130]

Burleigh, like Lyman, now realized that a sizable contingent of men had broken off from the main throng and filled in Wilson's Lane, forming a narrow chokepoint, where they had seized Garrison. Both men hustled toward the Old State House.

"They are going to hang him; for God's sake, save him!" Lyman heard as he rushed over to his office. He needn't ask whom they were referring to. As he approached the building, Lyman spotted Garrison, who was being led by two burly men and enveloped by an immense crowd.

One of the men gripping Garrison was Aaron "Buff" Cooley, a rowdy and rugged laborer from a working-class neighborhood. Cooley worked as a truckman, delivering and transporting goods, and was certainly no abolitionist.

In fact, a group of his fellow truckmen had recently written an anonymous letter to Garrison warning him to move his newspaper office and cease publishing the *Liberator*. "If it is issued again beware of yourself you will have a coat of tar and feathers and you will do well if you get your life saved," they wrote, promising no mercy. The letter was signed simply, "Thirty Truckmen," with no names attached.[131]

It's not known whether Cooley was one of the thirty truckmen, but his views generally aligned with them. Cooley had joined the rioters chasing Garrison to the carpentry shop and watched as he was dragged on Wilson's Lane. He saw the crowd jabbing at Garrison, grabbing at his clothes and clamoring for him to be delivered to the Boston Common to mete out his punishment. "Rush him to the Common and hang him," one voice was heard to cry.

You are hereby notified to remove your office and not to issue the paper any more. If it is issued again beware of yourself you will have a coats of tar and feathers and you will do well if you get your life saved. we shall have no mercy on you after this notification. Beware

Thirty Truckmen

pr C. Adams secty.

Please show Mr Garrison & Thompson this

Opposite: An artist's depiction of Garrison being dragged by the mob. *Library Company of Philadelphia.*

Right: This unsigned letter to Garrison threatened a "coat of tar and feathers" if he did not cease publishing the *Liberator*. BPL.

The sight of the pale, defenseless and disheveled Garrison struck a chord with Cooley; he now felt things had gone too far. Along with another friend, or possibly his brother Daniel, the muscular Cooley jumped into the fray and, with a powerful thrust, knocked down the man clutching Garrison's rope. He grabbed the abolitionist and escorted him down Wilson's Lane, acting as a bodyguard to keep the mob at bay. At one point, a man swung a club savagely at Garrison's head, but Cooley managed to ward off the blow.[132]

Cooley's role as the abolitionist's friend or foe was not totally clear. Several witnesses and spectators supported the view that Cooley acted as a protector, including Maria Chapman's younger brother. He recounted the story to one of his sisters, who wrote of Garrison's rescue "by an enormous truckman of the name of Aaron Cooley, who took him up in his arms and lifted him as high as he could and trampled the crowd with all fury."[133]

Garrison himself was less certain and later criticized Cooley for attempting to profit from his actions by soliciting funds from prominent abolitionist supporters. "You were neither an acquaintance or friend of mine, nor in the favor of the Anti-Slavery movement," he said later.[134]

The scrum advanced to the open expanse on the south side of the Old State House, where the crowds converged and thickened. Some witnesses estimated the crowd at up to five thousand, mostly well-dressed men, though not all were actively on the offensive; some were curiosity seekers or spectators like Wendell Phillips.

One young man who was working around the corner heard the hubbub and decided to venture out of his office to investigate. He encountered a "venerable" gentleman dressed in handsome attire nearby and asked what was happening.

"It is that God damned Garrison!" the gentleman answered, pointing to the center of the crowd.

The man looked and spotted the hatless and red-faced Garrison tethered to a rope and assumed he must be a murderer, pirate or robber. "What has he been doing, that he should be treated in this way?" he asked.

"Doing!" the gentleman replied in a rage. "Why the damned rascal has been holding a meeting in favor of the damned n------, but we've got him now and shall run him off the end of Long Wharf and drown the damned scoundrel," he exclaimed.[135]

Mayor Lyman circled around the building and confronted the crowd of gentlemen near the south entrance. Garrison was in his shirtsleeves, still in Buff Cooley's grasp at the time, and was staring down at the ground. He looked up when he heard Lyman, happy to see a friendlier face—or at least hear a friendly voice, since Garrison had lost his glasses and was quite farsighted. Although some claimed that Garrison appeared dejected and distraught, antislavery leaders maintained that he kept his composure the entire time.[136]

A local bank cashier named Charles Sprague spotted Garrison being dragged outside his office on State Street. He described the abolitionist as a man who "walked with head erect, calm countenance, flashing eyes, like a martyr going to the stake, full of faith and manly hope."[137] The lyrical language was no accident. While he worked as a cashier, Sprague also liked to write poetry and was known as the "Banker Poet" of Boston.

Mayor Lyman preferred to speak in prose. "Take him to my office," he ordered his constables.

Lyman stepped forward to assert himself but struggled to control the scene. Many in the crowd wanted to press on and deliver Garrison to the Boston Common for his tarring and feathering. "To the Frog Pond with him!" one voice called out.[138] Others were satisfied to deliver him to the mayor's custody, not wanting to see blood shed on the streets of Boston, just steps away from the site of the deadly Boston Massacre.

Garrison himself later pointed out the irony that he was violently dragged across the same ground that was stained with the blood of Revolutionary

Patriots fighting for the cause of liberty in 1770. "My offence was in pleading for liberty—liberty for my enslaved countrymen, colored though they be—liberty of speech and of the press for ALL!" he wrote.[139]

Aided by his constables and a handful of bystanders, the mayor finally succeeded in prying Garrison loose from the crowd. He escorted him to the south entrance of the building and up the handful of steps. In the process, Lyman nearly tripped over another man while ascending the stairs. As soon as Garrison crossed the threshold into the Old State House, Lyman stuck out his palm and pushed back on those who might try to follow him inside. "You can go no farther," he declared.[140]

The crowd obliged, though Garrison's apparent rescue angered many of them. The rioters still wanted their pound of flesh and now felt cheated. A group of men ran around to the north side of the building facing Washington Street and managed to get inside.

The first floor of the Old State House hosted the post office, merchants' exchange and Topliff's News Room, a reading room for Boston merchants. The mayor had Garrison carried upstairs to a room adjacent to the alderman's council, and he stood as a sentry at the base of the winding stairs. He cautioned the men who rushed in and filled the lower hall that law and order must be maintained.

The crowd inside was rowdy but stood down for the moment after hearing the mayor's admonition. Outside at the south entrance it was different story; the hordes continued to intensify. Lyman realized he needed to take action to defuse the situation or the rioters were likely to break in and overrun the building. He walked over to the small balcony above the south entrance and stood out on the ledge to address the crowd, holding on to the window frame with one hand to steady himself. It was a spot where official proclamations were often read to the public.

The mayor was fired up and made his determination known. Any attempt to force entry into the building would be over his own body, he said emphatically, and commanded the mob to disperse and return home. "The laws must and should be obeyed," he said.

The nearby spectators seemed receptive to the mayor's message, and some hearty cheers and applause could be heard over the hissing, hooting and boos. Small pockets of men spoke in groups in quieter tones as they digested the latest developments and decided what to do next.

Not everyone was impressed. Wendell Phillips was appalled at what he saw and critical of the mayor's generally hands-off approach with the mob, comparing him to a beggar. "Mayor Lyman besought instead of commanding that day, and was, metaphorically speaking, on his knees to the mob," he wrote much later.[141]

Still, most witnesses agreed that the mayor's remarks were delivered forcefully and conveyed the proper sense of urgency to the crowd. Josiah Quincy Jr., the president of the city council, agreed, praising Lyman's "prompt and spirited interference" in support of Garrison.[142] And yet the hostility still ran deep. One spectator recalled overhearing a group of men bragging that there was no place for Garrison to hide and they would drag him out of the building "as a cat would drag out a squirrel."[143]

Mayor Lyman was pleased with his remarks and their reception, but as he found a moment to catch his breath, his anxieties returned. Despite new developments, the scene now playing out was all too familiar. Garrison, the despised abolitionist, was trapped inside a building with a large group assembled outside looking to do him harm. Little had changed since the afternoon. The Old State House was perhaps better suited to offer protection than the antislavery office, but they were essentially back in the same position—except now it was growing dark.

"The moment was critical," Lyman explained. If Garrison was kept in the building overnight, there would be "great tumult," he feared.[144]

It was time to come up with a plan.

Chapter 10

ALL'S FAIR

Persons are requested not to handle the articles, which, like slavery, are too "delicate" to be touched.

After their harrowing journey and brief stop at the home of Francis Jackson, Maria Chapman invited her fellow members of the Boston Female Anti-Slavery Society to her own home to conduct their meeting, Susan Paul likely among them. Chapman was determined not to let these Boston men of property and standing divert them from their mission. This was supposed to be their annual meeting, and there was still business to be done.

The group's second annual antislavery fair was planned for December, and it was an important event: the proceeds helped support the New England Anti-Slavery Society's broader mission. The year before, in mid-December, the women had held their first holiday fair at the antislavery offices, the same location from which they had just fled under mob assault. By all accounts, the event had been a great success for an inaugural effort, raising more than $300 despite limited attendance.

The one-day fair, with an admission price of twelve cents, offered a range of handmade goods, crafts and ornaments, including quilts, iron holders, bowls, bags, baskets, needle-books, flags, linens and shrubs. A group of Black women from Salem contributed a number of articles to be sold. Many of the items had clever abolition-themed takes, such as the pot holders marked as "anti-slave holders," a sugar bowl boasting of "sugar not made by slaves" and a flag with "stripes on the banner, none on the back."[145] A sign posted inside the hall for the event mocked the proslavery attitudes held by much of the Boston establishment: "Persons are requested not to handle the articles, which, like slavery, are too 'delicate' to be touched."

Susan Paul had played a key role in organizing and hosting the fair and was singled out for praise in the *Liberator* after the fact. "Although she had a colored complexion, yet, in all that constitutes female excellence, she has not her superior in the republic," the paper wrote. Paul was helping to spearhead the event again this year, which would be expanded to a two-day sale, and Maria Chapman and her sisters were also heavily involved.[146]

Hosting the fair at the antislavery rooms on Washington Street did not seem wise under the present circumstance, and the women may have been discussing alternate locations during their reconvened meeting at Chapman's home.[147]

The conversation was soon interrupted by an unexpected visitor, who arrived pale and out of breath. It was not good news. Dr. Amos Farnsworth, an abolitionist from the town of Groton, had been at the women's meeting with Henry Chapman. He left the antislavery hall at the same time as the women but had remained out in the street.

Garrison was now in the hands of the mob, he told the women excitedly, and recounted how his friend was dragged through the streets and battered with violent blows aimed at his head. It would be a miracle if he escaped, Farnsworth told them. He also counseled the women that if George Thompson was still there, he should leave town right away. The women were distressed to learn the news.

For Susan Paul, the news hit especially hard. She and her family had grown close to Garrison over the years. After her father's death in 1831, Garrison had taken on her younger brother as an apprentice at the *Liberator*. Young Thomas Paul spent nearly four years at the paper learning the trade and then headed off to continue his education at a new interracial high school in New Hampshire founded by abolitionists.[148]

Garrison went out of his way to promote Susan Paul's juvenile choir performances and supported her many antislavery and social reform efforts. He had also comforted her when tragedy struck in June. Her older sister, Anne Catherine, died unexpectedly at age twenty-seven of "lung fever" (pneumonia), leaving several young children to care for, including an infant.[149] For the unmarried Paul, with a younger brother and already widowed mother, her sister's death presented both a familial and financial hardship.

An advertisement for Susan Paul's *Memoir of James Jackson. From the* Liberator.

Despite it all, Paul had just completed a remarkable project. She researched, wrote and published a biography chronicling the life of a young Black boy named James Jackson who was a student in her school: *The Memoir of James Jackson, the Attentive and Obedient Scholar, Who Died in Boston, October 31, 1833, Aged Six Years and Eleven Months.*

The memoir, newly published in May 1835, offered a window into the life of an inspirational young boy whose strong religious faith and spiritual health guided him through a life of challenges. Her didactic narrative was aimed at a younger audience, but there was also a broader message, one that Paul likely channeled through her own experiences confronting racism.[150]

"Let, then, this little book do something towards breaking down that unholy prejudice which exists against color," she wrote in her introduction. "These children of our brethren have too long been neglected. There is among them many a gem, and whose is the guilt that they are not brought out from among the rubbish and polished?"[151]

Paul prepared the manuscript and tried to have it published but met with some initial resistance. One of the leading religious publishers refused to publish or stock the book, no doubt due to its antislavery and pro-abolitionist sentiments. Instead, a local bookseller named James Loring stepped forward and paid for it to be published. Copies were sold at his shop on Washington Street and at the antislavery offices. The *Liberator* published excerpts from the book and promoted it liberally, and copies also found their way to abolitionist-friendly outlets and Sunday schools in New York and elsewhere.

The memoir was favorably received.[152] "It shows that remarkable intelligence, and remarkable moral integrity and excellence, may exist under color of a colored skin, as well as under any other," said one newspaper review.[153] The writer was referring to young James, but the words could have equally applied to Susan Paul.

After learning of Garrison's capture, Chapman felt it was best to adjourn their meeting once and for all. There was also fear that the mob might turn its attention back to the society and come looking for trouble at Chapman's home. The women decided it was best to leave one by one so as not to attract more attention.

Susan Paul left the Chapmans and headed back to her own home in the North Slope section of Beacon Hill, a segregated neighborhood that stood in the literal (and figurative) shadows of the Massachusetts State House. The cramped wooden buildings and boardinghouses stood in stark contrast to the stately rowhouses that composed the wealthy South Slope, where much of the Boston establishment lived, including Wendell Phillips's family.

Paul probably avoided crossing through the Boston Common, where some of the mob were still loitering. The lower end of the Common, which abutted her neighborhood, also boasted a fertile array of smells. The area was adjacent to an old salt marsh, once used as a town dump, and was still home to a burial ground and the occasional grazing cow, despite a recently passed city ordinance designed to regulate pasturage.[154]

She may have passed by the amphitheater on the Common, which only a few months prior had hosted an unusual event to celebrate the Fourth of July: the launching of a hot air balloon. A balloonist and his young son, using hydrogen gas, lifted off from the Common and traveled as high as five thousand feet over Cambridge and the Boston Harbor Islands, eventually touching down safely in East Boston.

A more common sight on Paul's walk home was the African Meeting House, the Federal-style red brick building built and financed with Black labor, where her father had famously preached for many years before his death. It was here that the seeds of her social reform were planted as a young teenager, where she was influenced by pioneering antislavery activists David Walker and Maria Stewart.

The building also served as the birthplace of the New England Anti-Slavery Society. It was a stormy evening in January 1832 when twelve white abolitionists gathered in the basement to formally approve a charter and constitution calling for immediate emancipation of all enslaved people. Afterward, Garrison remarked on the historical significance of the new organization.

"We have met tonight in this obscure school-house; our numbers are few and our influence limited; but mark my prediction, Faneuil Hall shall ere long echo with the principles we have set forth. We shall shake the nation with our mighty power," he said.[155]

Susan Paul had not been present at this formative meeting, though she now served on the society's board and had become one of its most active members. As darkness fell and she scurried home to escape the proslavery mob now flooding the streets of Boston, the powerful words of Garrison, though heartfelt, must yet have seemed quite empty.

Chapter 11

THE GAUNTLET

Escape seemed a physical impossibility. They clung to the wheels—dashed open the doors—seized hold of the horses—and tried to upset the carriage.

While the mayor and his advisors huddled, Garrison took a moment to clean up. His entire journey from the antislavery office to the carpentry shop to the Old State House had covered fewer than two hundred yards, but he'd taken quite a beating in the process. His clothes were ripped, torn and frayed, and he'd lost his jacket, hat and glasses.

A friendly visitor offered him a fresh pair of pants, while others outfitted him with a new coat and cap. His friend Samuel Sewall also paid a visit and was pleased to see that Garrison remained steadfast and clear-headed despite the physical abuse.

"I have seldom seen him in such high spirits, though he had just escaped from the hands of ruffians, and the same bloodthirsty wretches then surrounded the hall and were only waiting for the darkness of night…to make a general assault on the building and wreak their vengeance on him," Sewall recalled.

Vengeance was also a concern for Mayor Lyman. After talking it over with his constables and Deputy Sheriff Daniel Parkman, they decided the safest place for Garrison for the night would be the city jail on Leverett Street. But in order to lawfully commit him, they would need to file a formal charge.

Depiction of rioters seizing Garrison. *From the* Anti-Slavery Record, *September 1836.*

Sheriff Parkman drafted a complaint for disturbing the peace. Selling it to Garrison was another story. As a matter of logic, he understood that his life remained in danger and his continued presence in the building put everyone in jeopardy. But he was a man of principles, and going to jail and having a complaint sworn out against him was a tough pill to swallow.

Reluctantly, Garrison agreed to go, but not without a warning to the mayor: "I am in your hands. It is your business to protect me. If you see fit to take me to the jail I consent, but remember the responsibility is yours not mine!" he warned.[156]

Lyman said later that Garrison agreed to be committed to the jail only on condition that he not be subject to any expense, though the accuracy of the claim was disputed. Garrison himself would only say that he felt he had no say in the matter. "It is true, I made no objection, because freedom of choice did not appertain to my situation," he explained later.[157]

Parkman completed the paperwork. His formal complaint alleged that Garrison did "unlawfully, riotously…assemble, and then and there did disturb and break the peace of the Commonwealth, and a riot did cause and make, to the terror of the good people of the Commonwealth, and against the peace and dignity of the same."

Garrison was not aware at the time that his warrant and detention were based on the criminal charge. Had he known this, it's likely he would have objected more strenuously or even rejected the offer outright. As it was, the complaint was duly authorized by a justice of the peace, and Garrison was ordered held in jail.

Getting him there would be no simple task. The jail was located nearly a mile away on Leverett Street in the West End, close to the Charles River. Just getting Garrison out of the building safely would be a challenge, much less transporting him across town with plenty of chokepoints and potential roadblocks to surmount.

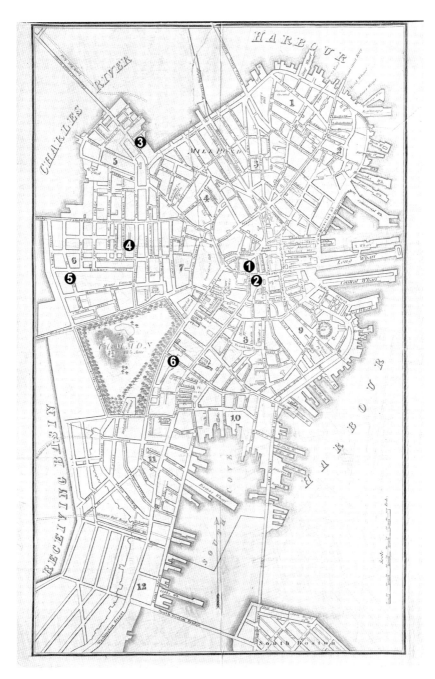

1) The antislavery office on Washington Street; 2) The Old State House; 3) Leverett Street Jail; 4) African Meeting House; 5) Susan Paul's family home; 6) Maria Chapman's home. *Original map from BPL.*

To overcome the first obstacle, Mayor Lyman decided to engage in subterfuge. He ordered a horse-drawn coach to be stationed outside the south entrance of the building where Garrison had first entered and then sent out his constable and a pair of city officials. The men spoke to the driver and then opened the carriage door. Another official ordered the crowd to stand back away from the horses, and a small cadre formed a double line to guard the short path from the door of the building to the coach. The activity attracted the attention of the crowd, which assumed Garrison was about to make his getaway.

While this was happening, another coach quietly drove up to the north entrance of the Old State House. The mayor and the sheriff grabbed Garrison—who was now dressed in new clothes, which helped disguise his appearance—and escorted him to the north side door. Lyman hoped the distraction on the opposite side of the building would divert attention long enough for them to get Garrison safely away.

A few of the spectators spotted the activity and figured out what was happening. "When the noise and confusion was greatest on the south side, the door of the north side was quickly opened, and an officer came out with a person by the arm and jumped into the coach," one witness said.

Lyman's ruse worked—briefly—but the distracted crowd soon discovered what was happening and rushed back toward the north entrance "like a mighty wall of water in a Western canyon," according to one witness.[158]

As Garrison exited the building and attempted to get in the coach, he was led by Sheriff Parkman and a man named Ebenezer Bailey. Bailey, age forty and some six feet tall, was a city councilor and ran the progressive school for young women where Maria Chapman had worked. Though he "shared the pro-slavery sentiment of the time," he was sympathetic to Garrison's plight and did his best to fend off the rioters now rushing in their direction.[159]

"I had with me a large, strong umbrella, and as we tried to get [Garrison] into the carriage, there was such a rush made upon him that I struck with my whole strength in every direction," Bailey recalled. The force of his umbrella parry broke the arm of one of the unlucky rioters, according to a story later told by Maria Chapman's sister.[160]

Garrison got inside the coach safely, but the mob, newly enraged by the attempted deception, was not done with him. A group of "neatly dressed young men," mostly merchant clerks, grabbed at the carriage wheels and tried to overturn the coach, while another tried to cut the harness rigging and command the two horses.[161] "Cut the traces! Cut the reins!" one man with a knife yelled out, until he was subdued. The vehicle was quickly surrounded by a dense mass of people.

"Escape seemed a physical impossibility," Garrison recalled. "They clung to the wheels—dashed open the doors—seized hold of the horses—and tried to upset the carriage."

Garrison was not the only one who feared the worst. His friend Samuel Sewall watched the scene with growing alarm. "For some moments I felt very doubtful whether Garrison would not again be in the hands of the wild beasts who surrounded the carriage," he said.[162] Another witness, observing the "ferocity" of the crowd's expression, felt certain that the abolitionist would be killed if the mob got their hands on him.[163]

Mayor Lyman's constables managed to repel most of the rioters and secure Garrison inside the coach—though Sheriff Parkman was not able to accompany him in the carriage as planned—but no sooner had they done so than another threat emerged: one of the rioters had taken the same rope that Garrison was earlier tethered to and swung it around the carriage body in an attempt to overturn the vehicle.

The man yanked on the line and succeeded in lifting the carriage wheels off the ground. For a moment, it appeared the entire coach, with Garrison inside, would be flipped over. Thinking quickly, the driver cracked his whip, and the frightened horses sprang forward, overpowering the man with the rope who had to let go.

Josiah Fuller, the young barber who had chased Garrison near the carpenter's shop, decided to jump into the fray. He grabbed a long leather strap hanging from the back of the carriage and jumped aboard.[164] He was joined by other young men, and their collective weight slowed the vehicle's acceleration.

The coach driver, with "good horses and good courage," cracked the whip, and the carriage wheels started turning. They lurched forward on Court Street, bursting through the crowd and trampling some of the rioters who hooted in protest.

To elude the mob, the driver decided to take a circuitous route to the jail and headed first for Bowdoin Square. Still, many of the rioters tried to race alongside and hamper their progress, and anytime the vehicle took a corner, more men would try to jump on and slow the horses. They might have succeeded in bringing the coach to a stop if it were not for a lucky assist from one of Garrison's friends.

James Buffum, an abolitionist who lived in the city of Lynn, about fifteen miles north, happened to be passing through Boston that day and heard about the attack on his friend. He was riding nearby in his chaise, a light carriage with a folding roof, and caught up to the coach on Court Street. Buffum could see that the vehicle was making slow progress due to the extra weight from all the young men dragging on the sides and rear. He maneuvered his chaise close alongside so that the two hubs of the carriage wheels were nearly touching. By doing so, several rioters were brushed off the side and fell, *splat*, to the ground, thus lightening the load. The driver cracked the whip on his team—and a few of the rioters' heads as well— and the horses accelerated to a full gallop. As the coach picked up speed, it veered left at Bowdoin Square and headed toward Cambridge Street, leaving a sizable contingent of the mob in its wake.[165]

Rioters continued to harass the coach as it navigated the patchwork of streets toward the jail, and there were several "hair-breadth" escapes. A twelve-year-old boy later recalled the carriage whooshing past him on Leverett Street with the mob still in pursuit. He noted that Garrison looked composed despite all the furor, and the young men in the crowd did not appear to be the "rough" sort.[166]

Mayor Lyman did not ride in the coach with Garrison but rather ran most of the way on foot. He was not alone. By the time Lyman arrived at the jail, a crowd of two or three hundred men had gathered. Because the coach driver took a winding route to evade the mob, Lyman arrived at the jail before Garrison.

When the coach pulled up in front, Lyman and his constables formed a line of defense to hold off the rioters, bolstered by the presence of some of Garrison's friends. As soon as the vehicle stopped, Garrison jumped out of the door and bounded for the jail entrance. The rioters swarmed forward from both sides of the street.

One of them was Josiah Fuller, who had clung to the leather strap on the back of the carriage for the entire ride. "I saw Garrison escape from the carriage to the grim portal which was open awaiting his coming," he recalled.

As soon as the jail door swung closed behind him, Garrison let out a sigh of relief. He felt fortunate to have survived the gauntlet. "That it was successful is truly a marvel; for the scene around the carriage was indescribably perilous," he said.[167]

He hoped his fortunes would now turn for the better. "In a few moments I was locked up in a cell," he recalled, "safe from my persecutors, accompanied by two delightful associates, a good conscience and a cheerful mind."[168]

Chapter 12

BROADCLOTH BYSTANDERS

These women opened my eyes.

The spectacle outside the Old State House began to calm soon after Garrison's departure, and within an hour the rowdy crowds had mostly dispersed. Some of the rabble reassembled around the jail, others caroused on the Common and some migrated to nearby taverns, wine cellars and coffeehouses to cap off a long day of rioting by quaffing pints of porter and ale.

Wendell Phillips may have returned to his law office on Court Street before heading home or joined the other young attorneys who practiced in his building to confer on the riotous scene they had just witnessed. The day's events had left Phillips feeling deeply unsettled. While some of the working-class ruffians were unskilled laborers, many of the gentlemen rallying and rioting in the streets in their broadcloth, camlet coats, cassimeres, and beaver hats were his own peers. The sartorial splendor of the crowd certainly stood out. "I have kept a hat store thirty years and never saw so many good hats before in my life," one local hat seller later remarked.[169]

Phillips did not agree with, or even understand, the abolitionist movement, yet the open contempt and defiance of the laws, the disorder, the lawlessness ran counter to his own cherished beliefs. It was his first lesson of the inadequacy of republican institutions, he later said.[170]

Phillips was especially dismayed to see how the women had been treated, unceremoniously evicted from their meeting and then paraded through the street in front of the mob. It was not until much later, however, that he fully realized the ramifications and the impact it had in shaping his own beliefs.

Still, Phillips's evolving views on the matter did not translate into any action; he'd remained a curious spectator, neither joining the fracas nor intervening to allay it. One critic later pointed out as much, recognizing some who aided the cause of law and order, while noting that men like Phillips had sat on their hands: "Mr. Phillips was hanging his head in shame; which act seems to be the only support he gave to the law and the authorities on that…occasion."[171]

Phillips was not the only one who met the moment with meekness. Representative Ellis Ames, the young legislator from West Bridgewater, left the scene outside city hall and stopped to pay a visit at the law office of Rand & Fiske on the corner of Washington and Court Streets. One of the law partners, Augustus Fiske, had watched the mob from his window the entire time and "complained bitterly that there was not better and safer means to prevent a murder by a mob in the street."

Soon after, Ames left Rand & Fiske and crossed the street to visit another young attorney, Charles Sumner, who had been cooped up in his office most of the afternoon. Number 4 Court Street, where Sumner and his law partner shared adjoining offices on the second floor, was also home to a cadre of prominent and aspiring lawyers, including Horace Mann, Rufus Choate and Edward Loring.[172]

Surprisingly, Sumner did not seem to be aware of all the hubbub, though his office connected via a short passage to a south-facing window that

overlooked the plaza. Ames quickly filled him in on all the developments, but the young lawyer did not "express such anxiety about the affair as Mr. Fiske did," Ames recalled.[173] Had Ames not recounted the scene first, Sumner's father likely would have; Charles Pinckney Sumner was Suffolk County sheriff and had assisted in escorting Garrison safely from the Old State House to the jail.

The young Sumner may have been more sympathetic to the antislavery cause than his friend Wendell Phillips—mostly due to his father's influence—but he did not consider himself an abolitionist and said later that he considered the *Liberator* "vindictive, bitter and

Charles Sumner, circa 1846. *National Park Service.*

unchristian."[174] At this early juncture of his career, Sumner's passion was for literature and the scholarly side of the law; his legal writings rarely delved into the political realm or any social causes.

Though he professed little interest in the cause and did not directly witness the rioting, the day's events clearly had an impact on Sumner, as they did with Phillips. Two and a half months later, he wrote to a friend acknowledging as much: "We are becoming abolitionists at the North fast; the riots, the attempts to abridge the freedom of discussion…have caused many to think favorably of immediate emancipation who never before inclined to it," he wrote.[175]

Henry Bowditch, a promising young physician who had an office nearby, also watched the rioting from the street corner. He knew little of Garrison or the antislavery cause; his own interests were in the medical field, where he was quickly developing expertise in diseases of the chest.

Dr. Bowditch watched the scene with naive curiosity. Why were these respectable gentlemen acting in such a contemptible way, like "sans culottes," he asked one city official he encountered. The response surprised him: while it was the mayor's duty to quell the mob, the city did not much appreciate Garrison, or the abolitionists, and was rather happy to see them get a comeuppance.[176] Bowditch frowned in disgust. Another seed had been planted.

Edmund Quincy, an attorney whose father was a former mayor and eponymous advocate of Quincy Market, also watched from his office on State Street. That evening, he attended a Beacon Hill soîrée, but there was little talk of rioting; instead, his dinner conversation focused on European wedding tours.[177]

Charles Francis Adams, son of the former president, was another prominent young Boston attorney who shared offices on Court Street near Sumner, Phillips and the others. While he didn't agree with slavery, Adams felt at the time that the issue of abolitionism was one that was "wiser not to touch." He took a pause from his regular legal and political writings to briefly note the mob rioting in his daily diary. "Among other things we have had a mob to put down Abolitionists, as if the Country was not going to pot fast enough without extraordinary help," he remarked wryly.[178]

If many of the leading young men of Boston were, on this day at least, apathetic, Maria Chapman and the women of the antislavery society were apoplectic. After their meeting broke up, Chapman remained at her home on West Street to wait for news of Garrison and busied herself with needlepoint.

Her anger at the rioters and city leaders and her anxiety for Garrison's well-being were tempered by her faith in knowing that her cause was a righteous one. If the cost was a "baptism of suffering," she was prepared to pay it.[179] She felt gratified that a number of women had banded with them in their march from the antislavery office and joined the group, knowing the perils they faced. These women had already demonstrated their fidelity to the cause, she felt.

"We rejoiced over them, more than over the sixty that joined our ranks in more favorable times," she later wrote.

A steady throng of visitors passed by Chapman's house that afternoon and evening—some friendly, others less welcome. At one point, the mob threatened to make a move against them, under the assumption that George Thompson had taken sanctuary there.

Maria took the precaution of sending her two young children away for the evening and removing her picture of George Thompson on display. Her sisters Anne and Caroline left her house between four and five o'clock after the visit from Dr. Farnsworth. They headed back home in great distress after learning about Garrison's brush with death at the hands of the mob.

Chapman's younger brother Warren, an excitable sixteen-year-old who shared his father's fondness for liquor, had left the house around teatime and returned sometime after his sisters departed. He delivered the welcome news that Garrison had been rescued from the mob with help from a brawny truckman and was now safely deposited at the jail.

As Warren updated his sister with the latest news, Henry Chapman went out to check on his parents' home a couple of blocks away on Chauncy Place. No sooner had he left than a pair of visitors came calling: Sheriff Parkman and Edward Prescott, a justice of the peace who had signed off on the complaint to commit Garrison to the jail. They came looking for Mr. Chapman, but Maria invited them in so they could wait for his return.

Rumors were still swirling that Thompson remained in the city, and Parkman and Prescott assumed the Chapmans might know something or even be sheltering him in their home. If that was the case, they had come to advise his "instant removal." Her husband may not have been present, but Maria Chapman was not shy about speaking her mind. The conversation was cordial in tone, but she made sure her views were known.

At one point, Prescott offered a condescending comment about his brushes with the mob, as if to emphasize the potential peril they were facing.

"I speak as a man just from a mob," he reminded her, but Maria Chapman would have none of that.

"And I listen as a *woman* just from a mob," she retorted.

After a lengthy conversation, Chapman led the men out, and they departed on friendly terms. It was now late into the evening on what had been a long and eventful day. The mob's actions and the city's inaction had left her both exercised and energized. She was probably ready for bed, but the night's drama was not quite over.

Chapter 13

VISITORS

My escape from death or outrages was marvelous indeed,
but no thanks to him.

After making sure that Garrison was safely inside the jail, Theodore
Lyman returned to his office at the Old State House that evening.
He alerted his night watch and assigned constables to stand out in
front of the *Liberator* newspaper office on Cornhill, around the corner from
the antislavery office. So far, things were quiet, but there were still pockets
of men roaming the area and stirring up trouble, and he wanted to head off
any more incidents.

Lyman also sent a constable to check on Garrison's home on Brighton
Street, another potential target of the mob. It was far afield from most of
the day's rioting, but he was fearful, nonetheless. As it turned out, there
was little to worry about. Mrs. Garrison wasn't even home; after being
escorted from the antislavery office in the afternoon, she went and stayed
with a friend.

In fact, a young Black woman who was a house guest of the Garrisons
seemed to be blissfully unaware of the pending drama when a visitor stopped
by earlier in the night. After answering the door, the young woman politely
advised the visitor that Mr. and Mrs. Garrison had gone out to attend a
meeting and would not be back until later in the evening. She "seemed as
unaware of the excitement which prevailed in the city as if she had been

living in the moon."[180] (The young woman may have been the daughter of Garrison's friend and financial backer John B. Vashon.)

By the time Mayor Lyman settled in, it was after eight o'clock. All in all, he was pleased with how he'd handled the situation. There was no loss of life, and property damage was minimal. As far as he could tell, it amounted to the antislavery sign, a wooden partition in the building and a broken door; at most, it was twenty dollars in damages.

"Garrison himself received no personal injury. His trousers were torn, and I believe he lost his hat," Lyman surmised.[181]

His deputy and constables had acted properly and with honor, Lyman felt. Sheriff Parkman in particular had shown courage in the face of a hostile crowd, and even when he was "roughly handled" a few times, he kept his cool under pressure.

Sitting in the Leverett Street Jail, Garrison did not share Mayor Lyman's cheerful diagnosis. Even by the standards of the day, the jail was not a pleasant place to be. The stone hewn structure, standing adjacent to the jail keeper's home, was run-down and poorly heated, and the building stank of foul air. The jail walls were bound with iron, and loose cannonballs were cemented in blocks as further security.

The Boston City Council had recently appropriated funds to make improvements and recommended reforms.[182] Just one week earlier, a man imprisoned for counterfeiting had committed suicide in the jail by cutting his throat with a razor, and behind the jail on the wharf was an area reserved for executions where five Spaniards had been hanged for crimes of piracy five months earlier.[183]

Garrison was relieved to be safe behind bars but indignant that a jail cell was the only apparent place of sanctuary in the city. He blamed Mayor Lyman for not doing more to quell the mob and restore order. These were his people, after all.

"If the mayor had done his duty I should not have left the hall that night until the rioters had dispersed, or he should have taken me to his house," Garrison thought. He blamed the mayor for sending him out of the Old State House to face the rioters on the perilous journey to the jail, where the odds of his safe arrival were "one to ninety-nine."[184]

"The mayor ought not to have subjected me to such a strong probability of my recapture. My escape from death or outrages was marvelous indeed, but no thanks to him," he wrote.[185]

Apart from his frustrations with the mayor, Garrison remained in good spirits. Like Maria Chapman, he was buoyed by his faith in the abolitionist cause and felt a deep sense of resolve. His mood was also lifted by a steady stream of visitors who came to check on him throughout the evening, speaking through a grated window in his cell.

One of them was John Greenleaf Whittier, an abolitionist writer and poet who had witnessed the crowd mobbing the women's antislavery meeting earlier in the day. His own wife, Elizabeth Whittier, was a member and was sitting upstairs in the hall with Maria Chapman, Susan Paul and the others when the drama first unfolded. Garrison joked with Whittier about the spartan quarters in the jail: "You see my accommodations are so limited, that I cannot ask you to spend the night with me."[186]

Amos Bronson Alcott and his wife, Abigail, both dedicated abolitionists, also stopped by the jail that evening to visit their friend. The Alcotts had just returned from a visit in the town of Concord, some twenty miles outside the city—making the acquaintance of a young writer and philosopher named Ralph Waldo Emerson—and missed the day's drama. The Alcotts reported that Garrison appeared "serene."[187]

Alcott's brother-in-law Samuel Sewall also visited Garrison and shared the upbeat report. "He seemed very cheerful. He was not at all injured, though his clothes were very much torn, when he was in the hands of the mob, and his hat lost," Sewall noted.[188]

Rounding up Garrison's cadre of visitors was Isaac Knapp, his business partner at the *Liberator* and a hometown friend. Knapp later reported to Mayor Lyman that Garrison felt he owed his life to the mayor for his efforts to protect him from the hands of the mob. The claim was later disputed and became a bone of contention among Garrison supporters.[189]

Garrison enjoyed chatting with his various visitors well into the evening and then retired to his spartan prison bed, where he slept "tranquilly" through the night.

Across town, Maria Chapman also had a steady stream of visitors, though they were not of the well-wisher variety. Sometime after ten o'clock, not long after the sheriff's departure, a contingent of four men came calling at the Chapman home. They included a pair of Mayor Lyman allies who were ringleaders of the mob: James Homer, the editor-in-chief of the *Boston Commercial Gazette*, and Henry Williams, the loud-mouthed, tobacco-chewing merchant who helped tear down the antislavery sign. Homer and Williams were joined by Benjamin Davenport, one of the men who conspired to produce the anti-Thompson handbill earlier in the day, and a fourth man whom Maria Chapman did not know.

Homer was surprised when Chapman told him she had sent her children away for safekeeping, a sign that he may not have realized the full extent of the hostilities his handbill had provoked. Chapman, too, may have been surprised by their visit, but she was nonetheless quite pleased to have an opportunity to give these men a piece of her mind. They were, after all, among those most responsible for causing the rioting. "The lord delivered them into her hand," one of her sisters later wrote.[190]

A common mission for visitors to the Chapman home throughout the evening was to learn the whereabouts of Thompson, one of the few abolitionists who could claim more detractors than Garrison. One abolitionist later recalled a conversation Chapman had with a group of men on the topic that evening, which may have been Homer and his contingent. The men came looking for Thompson and demanded to know if he was in their home.

"I know it," Chapman said, "and I know what you want with Mr. Thompson; you want his blood."[191]

The men denied it, but Chapman did not believe them, and she pressed for assurances. They first pledged not to shed his blood, and when that was not sufficient for her, they reluctantly gave their word that they would not cause Thompson any bodily harm.

"This pledge is what I wanted," Chapman declared, "and now I will tell you that Mr. Thompson is not here and I am sure I don't know where he is."

She continued to lay into the men with some choice words about how gentlemen ought to know better than to breach the peace and violate the laws of society. Her direct manner caught the men by surprise, unaccustomed as they may have been to hear a woman address them in this way. Her words had an impact on the men, though the effect was temporary. Their conversation was interrupted by the return of Henry Chapman, whose presence served to reignite the men's antagonism toward abolitionists.

The men warned Henry Chapman that they knew the names of his commercial trade customers in the South and were prepared to thwart his business dealings by outing his strident antislavery views. Chapman was undeterred by the blackmail threat and thanked the men for saving him the trouble. He and his father had already been cutting ties with southern trade partners who relied on the labor of enslaved persons, and earlier that week, they had declined a series of orders totaling some $3,000. Stymied in their threats and frustrated by their failure to find Thompson, the men finally left without further incident.

By the time Maria Chapman got to bed, it was close to midnight, if not later. It had been a long and exciting day—not just for herself but for the cause of abolition. Her younger sister summed it up in her diary entry that night: "This is to be remembered as the day 5,000 men mobbed 45 women."[192]

Chapter 14

JAILS AND RAILS

Give me brickbats in the cause of God, to wedges of gold in the cause of sin.

One of Garrison's first visitors to the jail on Thursday morning was his old friend John Vashon, who brought a welcome gift: a new fur hat to replace the one rioters had stolen and cut up with a knife. Garrison held the new hat up to admire and try on for size. He was pleased to see it was even the right fit.

Vashon, who was staying at Garrison's home for a few days, was no stranger to conflict. His barbershop in Pittsburgh had been attacked by a mob just two months earlier, and as a young man serving in the navy during the War of 1812, he'd been captured by the British during a battle off the coast of Brazil and held as a prisoner of war.[193]

After the war, Vashon moved from his native Virginia to Pennsylvania, first to Carlisle and later to Pittsburgh, where he opened a series of businesses, including one of the city's first public bathhouses. He soon became one of the city's wealthiest Black residents and most influential citizens, and his barbershop became a center for social reform and antislavery efforts.

There was a deep affection between the two men, and they exchanged letters often. Vashon was about a dozen years older and admired Garrison's passion for the antislavery cause and his drive for immediate emancipation. He generously supported the *Liberator* and acted as the newspaper's subscription agent in Pittsburgh. Like Garrison, Vashon was also an early opponent of the African colonization movement, which he described as a "scheme to drain the better-informed part of coloured people out of these United States so that the chain of slavery may be riveted more tightly."[194]

It was one of many links between the two men, though not all were apparent at the time. It is not known if Vashon's ten-year-old son George accompanied his father on this trip to Boston, but if he had, the young Vashon very well might have met his future wife, still an infant at the time.[195]

Along with the new hat and fresh clothes, Vashon offered some words of encouragement for Garrison in his jail cell. He may also have shared an update on Garrison's wife, who was safe at the home of a friend. Vashon was relieved to see his friend alive and well and seemingly in good spirits. He had witnessed much of the hostilities the day before and watched in fear as Garrison was dragged by the rope. He knew the horrors of war, and this type of mob violence hit too close to home.

After Vashon's visit and a full breakfast courtesy of the jail keep, Garrison took a moment to write an inscription on the wall of his prison cell. He intended to take full advantage of his near martyrdom to press the cause of abolition, knowing his words would long outlive his confinement:

> *Wm. Lloyd Garrison was put into this cell on Wednesday afternoon, Oct. 21, 1835, to save him from the violence of a "respectable and influential" mob, who sought to destroy him for preaching the abominable and dangerous doctrine, that "all men are created equal," and that all oppression is odious in the sight of God. "Hail, Columbia!" Cheers for the Autocrat of Russia and the Sultan of Turkey!*

It was not Garrison's first time behind bars. Before launching the *Liberator* in 1831, he had worked at an antislavery newspaper in Baltimore and had spent time in jail after being convicted of libel. Garrison's crime was penning an article attacking a shipping merchant for engaging in the slave trade. The ship owner hailed from his hometown of Newburyport, Massachusetts—a fact he found particularly odious—and was delivering seventy-five enslaved persons from Maryland to New Orleans. A Baltimore jury convicted Garrison of criminal libel, and the court imposed a fine of fifty dollars, which Garrison did not pay, resulting in his imprisonment. The ship owner filed civil charges as well, though he agreed to drop his suit in exchange for an apology—which, of course, Garrison also refused. Then, as now, Garrison wielded his righteousness as a sword to assail those who did not share his antislavery views.

Later that morning, Garrison was escorted out of his cell to stand before a judge. To avoid causing a spectacle or risking further violence, city officials decided not to bring him to the new courthouse located near the scene of the mob where the Boston Police Court usually presided. Instead, they led him behind the jail, through the yard and then up the back stairs of the old courthouse and into a private room.

It was about eleven o'clock when Garrison landed before Judge Benjamin Whitman, the sixty-seven-year-old chief justice. Sheriff Parkman was also present, along with a handful of city officials. There is no record of Mayor Lyman's appearance at the impromptu arraignment hearing.[196]

Two other men were also arraigned in police court that same day: a man named John Kelly for larceny charges and another, James Hemmenway, on a pair of assault charges. Neither man was in the room with Garrison, and their cases were probably handled at the new courthouse.[197] No one else was arraigned on rioting charges that day—a remarkable fact given the size of the mob. Most of the charges the police court dealt with that month included drunkenness, assault and larceny, with an occasional charge for "suffering a horse or dog to go at large."[198]

When the warrant was formally read before the judge, Garrison was angered to learn that he was charged with criminal disturbance of the peace. He knew the charges were a necessary fabrication to appease the mob and facilitate his safe transfer to the jail, but the distinction still irked him. It also gave him more rhetorical fodder to feast on, which he wasted little time in doing. "In my *false imprisonment* was seen another triumph of mob-law in the city of Boston!" he wrote soon after.[199]

The arraignment was brief. No witness or evidence was brought forward, and few other details were recorded on the court docket, likely a purposeful omission. The space on the docket that normally listed the name of the presiding constable was also left blank. Sheriff Parkman was listed as the sole witness. The consensus among city officials and Garrison's friends was that it was not safe for him to remain in the city, and all were anxious to see him depart without further delay.

After the brief hearing, an acquittal verdict was entered, and a standard court fee of $2.05 was set.[200] Garrison was quietly escorted back the way he had arrived, but in his haste, he neglected to retrieve his wallet and letters from the pocket of a coat he had borrowed while in the jail. He later posted a lost and found notice in the *Liberator* seeking their return.[201]

There were reports of men searching for Garrison (and Thompson) in stagecoaches departing Boston, so Sheriff Parkman instead drove him outside

The city court docket showing Garrison's arrest on the charge of rioting (entry #1899). Most of the charges the police court dealt with that month included drunkenness, assault and larceny, with an occasional charge for "suffering a horse or dog to go at large." *City of Boston Archives.*

the city, where he met up with his wife at the new Boston and Providence Railroad station in Canton.

Helen Garrison was relieved to finally see her husband safe. The previous afternoon, she'd tried to find him at the *Liberator* office and then later back at home. A bleak-faced visitor eventually shared the distressing news, and her first instinct was to rush out to find him. Her friends counseled that it was not wise for a young pregnant wife to be out among the masses, so she spent an anxious evening at the home of a family friend. Later, she learned that her husband had arrived safely at the jail, and her "heart swelled with gratitude." In spite of her own fears and the perils her husband surely must have faced, she took solace in their shared faith. "I know my husband will never betray his principles!" she said.[202]

The Garrisons boarded a train bound for Providence, Rhode Island, with plans to travel on to Brooklyn, Connecticut, to stay with Helen's family. While they headed southbound, possibly on one of the new steam-powered passenger locomotives, another member of the family was traveling in the opposite direction on the same tracks.

Garrison's brother-in-law and fellow abolitionist George W. Benson left Providence on Thursday afternoon bound for Boston after learning of the mob attack the previous day. Upon his arrival, he stopped by the Garrisons' home on Brighton Street to check in around six o'clock, unaware that he had already passed his sister and brother-in-law in transit. Garrison's friends soon filled him in, and Benson "was rejoiced to hear [he] had safely escaped these blood thirsty mobocrats."[203]

By Friday, the Garrisons had arrived at the family home, known as Friendship Valley, in Connecticut. Garrison's father-in-law "unexpectedly but cheerfully" welcomed their arrival. "I thought Boston was the last place that would suffer a riotous mob to annihilate law," he wrote his son, "and I ardently hope that a reaction friendly to the cause of justice may yet appear in that city."[204]

Garrison felt relief to be outside the city and know that his wife, Helen, some five months pregnant with their first child, was now out of harm's way. He'd visited his wife's family back in September, coinciding with the couple's first wedding anniversary, but did not expect to be back again so soon. His relief was tempered by a sense of anxiety about his affairs in Boston, the status of the *Liberator* and his friend George Thompson. "I am feverish to learn how he is now situated," he wrote.

Garrison knew his exile would give him an opportunity to spend more uninterrupted time for his writing, both for the *Liberator* and his regular correspondence. The hospitality of his in-laws also had the benefit of reducing his own household expenses and providing some needed financial relief. Still, almost immediately he yearned to be back in Boston and wondered how his absence would be perceived. He wrote to friends asking their advice about when he should return.

It did not sit well with him that the voices of the abolitionist movement in Boston were temporarily silenced and the mobocracy ascendant. He'd been through a harrowing experience, but he was at peace with himself and ready to jump back into to the lion's den if the cause required it.

"Give me brickbats in the cause of God, to wedges of gold in the cause of sin," he wrote.

Chapter 15

BLACK AND WHITE
AND READ ALL OVER

There is great fear among the brethren.

Despite not getting a full night of sleep, Maria Chapman woke up the morning after the riot feeling energized, telling her sister that "she never had such a delightful time in her life." The encounters with the mayor and the city's anti-abolitionist leaders gave her a platform to speak her mind, and she relished the opportunity. While Chapman remained anxious for the safety of her friends, the mob's attempts at intimidation had only served to strengthen her own voice—and, like Garrison, she was not afraid to play the martyr role if it helped advance the cause.

For the Weston sisters, the day was a mixture of excitement and apprehension. "Oh such an afternoon we passed yesterday; the morning was bad enough, but the hour between 5 and 6 was the most distressing and exciting I have ever passed in my life!" Chapman's sister Deborah wrote. In the afternoon, Anne Weston penned a brief letter to her aunt letting her know she was "safe & sound" and promised to share more news of the "very thrilling scene" soon.

The first newspaper accounts of the mob came out on Thursday— another unseasonably warm day—and Chapman was disappointed, though not surprised, to see the reaction. The establishment press in Boston was generally hostile, and most papers downplayed the mob's culpability, instead blaming the disturbance on the abolitionists. Chapman had confronted a number of men after the mob interruption, and many defaulted to chauvinistic attitudes in response.

One of the city's leading newspapers, the *Daily Advertiser and Patriot*, singled out Chapman's Anti-Slavery Society for criticism: "When women turn reformers and become so blinded by their zeal…it is incumbent on the officers of the law to step in, and preserve the public peace, and not wait until continued provocation shall have led to lawless acts of violence."[205]

The *Columbian Centinel*, a once influential Federalist newspaper that now backed the Whig Party, compared the female abolitionists to radical French revolutionaries, piling on with sexist insults: "Their husbands, fathers and guardians ought to keep them from meddling with public affairs of which they are ignorant."[206]

James Homer's *Commercial Gazette*, which had played such an active role in inciting the disturbance, emphasized the civility and manners displayed by the men gathered in the streets, or the "gentlemen of property and standing," as it famously dubbed them. The paper pointed out how the men cheerfully parted to allow women, Black and white alike, to exit safely. "We never before saw so gentlemanly a rabble—if a rabble it may be called—as that assembled yesterday."[207]

The plucky *Boston Atlas*, a Whig newspaper, dispensed with any pretense in the lead sentence of its blunt recap: "The abolitionists succeeded in producing another disturbance in our city yesterday."[208] Another Whig-leaning paper, the *Boston Mercantile Journal*, decried public lawlessness and called the riot disgraceful but blamed Garrison and Thompson for inciting it. "A meeting of the abolitionists is but a signal for the assemblage of a mob."[209]

While the rival Whigs and Democrats usually did not see to eye to eye on many issues—even the Whig-affiliated newspapers occasionally bickered about which paper was the *rightful* Whig Party organ—they shared a distaste for the cause of abolitionism. This shared view framed most of the negative coverage on both sides of the aisle, though the Whig Party domination in Boston was also reflected in the number of newspapers.

The *Morning Post*, one of the city's main Democratic papers, was a bit more muted in its finger pointing, heaping equal amounts of blame on the rioters as the abolitionists. "We deplore the madness of the abolitionists and condemn their measures; but still more do we deplore the fact that the city of Boston was yesterday a scene of violence and commotion."[210]

The abolitionists couldn't even catch a break from the religious press. The *Christian Watchman*, a Baptist newspaper, disapproved of the rioting and blamed both sides, including those who "persist in a course that is calculated to excite such proceedings." A congregationalist newspaper, the *Boston*

Recorder, offered similar criticism, calling Garrison a skilled martyr who sought to provoke turmoil.

One of the few supportive reactions came from the *Boston Daily Advocate*, a Democratic newspaper, which forcefully denounced the "men of property" who sanctioned the riot. "Shall the rich man be sent to the Leverett Street Jail to protect him in the enjoyment of his liberty?"[211]

Chapman was, of course, more concerned with another publication, the *Liberator*. The newspaper was regularly published on Saturdays, and that schedule was now in jeopardy. The *Liberator* office was sandwiched among a cluster of booksellers, print shops and publishers on Cornhill, a short distance from the antislavery offices. There were reports of rioters canvassing outside the office on Wednesday evening, and the mayor had assigned men to patrol the area. Garrison's friend Charles Burleigh also took the precaution of removing the *Liberator*'s books and petty cash from the office.

So far, there had been no further reports of physical violence or vandalism, but that had not prevented jittery landlords and neighboring tenants from raising objections. The owner of the building that housed the *Liberator* office informed them he wanted the newspaper out right away, and since there was no lease, there was little that could be done. Even an attempt to fasten a temporary sign on the front door of the nearby antislavery office had engendered objections from the first-floor tenants.[212]

For the *Liberator*, the ripple effect was felt almost immediately; creditors and vendors stepped forward seeking payment, and quickly, the newspaper was $600 in the hole. Finding a new space would not be easy in the current climate, and so plans were devised to divvy up the newspaper's supplies and materials and store them in separate locations while a more permanent office was scouted.

With Garrison out of state, Chapman and other friends did what they could to assist in getting the next *Liberator* to press. Burleigh began writing a first-person account of the riot for publication, and others went to work on the next issue under the direction of Isaac Knapp, who temporarily covered the paper's debt personally. Still, Burleigh remained apprehensive. "The affairs of the *Liberator* are somewhat crippled," he explained in a letter to Garrison.[213]

Burleigh was more optimistic on the broader matter of the abolitionist movement. Like Chapman, he felt the mob's brazen actions would backfire and bolster support for their cause in the long run. "I think we have reason to believe it has made us friends," he said. Knapp echoed that sentiment, telling Garrison of new supporters who may not have shared

Thompson knew his letter would later be published, and it was clearly intended for a broader audience than just Garrison. While writing it, he brought down installments and read them aloud in front of the Southwicks to judge their reaction and solicit feedback. Young Sarah Southwick was duly impressed and still recalled his eloquence many years later.[225]

Chapter 16

JUSTICE GONE SOUTH

We predict, if the abolitionists do not succumb,
that they will meet, at home, an awful punishment.

The morning after the riot, Mayor Lyman returned to his office in the Old State House. He was exhausted by the frenetic pace of events from the preceding afternoon and evening but pleased to see that the early newspaper accounts had favorable things to say about the city's handling of the mob. He felt he and his deputies had handled a difficult situation as best as could be expected.

Lyman had already decided that he would not be running again in December, and so his term as Boston mayor would be ending in two and a half months. His legacy and reputation were of paramount importance, and he was proud of his efforts to prevent violence and protect Garrison, even though he did not much care for the man or his radical causes.

Among the visitors to the mayor's office on Thursday morning was Isaac Knapp, accompanied by another man. The men had a lengthy conversation about the riot, and Knapp shared an update on his meeting with Garrison at the jail the night before.

Knapp was complimentary of the mayor's actions and recounted that Garrison also had praised his peacekeeping role. "[Garrison] considered that he owed his life to the exertions I made to rescue him from the hands of the mob," Lyman recalled Knapp saying during the morning meeting.[226] The same sentiment was echoed by Sheriff Parkman later in the day, probably after he returned from delivering Garrison to the train station.

After conversing with other city officials, it was decided not to pursue criminal charges against any of the ringleaders of the mob, though it was certainly not hard to identify who had been most responsible. In the end, the mob caused little actual property damage, apart from the antislavery sign, and Garrison had emerged physically unscathed, despite some close calls. Then there was a more practical matter: there was simply no political appetite to prosecute the city's most prominent residents.

Judge Joseph Story, the venerated Massachusetts jurist and law professor of Wendell Phillips, echoed those concerns. When asked by city leaders, he advised them that it would be best not to take any formal notice of the mob outrage given the strong feeling on the slavery issue.[227] His sentiment was prevalent throughout much of Boston.

Harriet Martineau, the British writer and reformer, was visiting the Boston area at the time and was surprised and dismayed by the level of enmity and intolerance she found toward the abolitionists and their cause. It was as if the city just did not want men like Garrison to live among them, she felt.

"Lawyers on that occasion defended a breach of the laws; ladies were sure that the gentlemen of Boston would do nothing improper: merchants thought the abolitionists were served quite right," she observed.

Martineau recounted a conversation with several prominent Bostonians, including a university president and a prominent attorney, soon after the riot. To her surprise, the men dismissed the idea that there had even been an actual mob:

> *"O, there was no mob,"* said [the attorney]. *"I was there myself, and saw they were all gentlemen. They were all in fine broad-cloth."*
>
> *"Not the less a mob for that,"* I said.
>
> *"Why, they protected Garrison. He received no harm. They protected Garrison."*
>
> *"From whom, or what?"*
>
> *"O, they would not really hurt him. They only wanted to show that they would not have such a person live among them,"* [the attorney replied].
>
> *"Why should not he live among them? Is he guilty under any law?"*
>
> *"He is an insufferable person to them."*
>
> *"So may you be to-morrow. If you can catch Garrison breaking the laws, punish him under the laws. If you cannot, he has as much right to live where he pleases as you."*[228]

Martineau reported that similar sentiments were expressed among the wealthier classes, but outside the city and among the working classes and younger generation, the views were generally more sympathetic or at least less hostile. She singled out the corrupting influence of trade as the major point of distinction. Her encounters motivated her to learn more about the cause of abolition, and she agreed to attend a future meeting.

Like the others, Wendell Phillips saw all the newspapers and heard the chatter among his fellow Court Street colleagues and Brahmin neighbors. His reaction fell somewhere in between Martineau and Mayor Lyman. The mob's actions violated his ingrained sense of fair play and left him feeling conflicted. He was not quite ready to rush out and subscribe to the *Liberator* as some others did, but his transition had begun, and many years later, he would remember the day as the first time he "touched the point of Radicalism."[229]

When Phillips read over the newspapers that week, the Boston mob was not the only one to catch his attention. In Utica, New York, on the same day that Garrison was attacked, a group of about eighty well-dressed men, mostly lawyers, bankers and merchants, broke into the inaugural meeting of the New York State Anti-Slavery Society at a local Presbyterian church. The mob succeeded in halting the proceedings and presenting their formal resolutions in protest, but there was no real violence or significant property damage, and the four hundred or so abolitionists regrouped the next day in another location.[230]

Just two days later, a mob interrupted a meeting of an antislavery society in Montpelier, Vermont, with hissing, shouts and stamping. The women in the audience departed, and the featured speaker, Reverend Samuel J. May, was unable to deliver his lecture. Reverend May traveled to Burlington the next day for another scheduled lecture but then changed plans and returned to Boston when he heard about the mob incident with his friend Garrison.[231]

The spate of mob activity drew attention across the country, particularly in the South, where Garrison, Thompson and the women's antislavery society members were viewed as fanatics. Most southern newspapers felt the mob attacks were entirely justified—and necessary—and the fact that they were led by gentlemen of "property and standing" was taken as an encouraging sign that the northern establishment backed southern slavery rights.

One Georgia newspaper summed up the views of much of the region toward abolitionists: "The people in the South cannot well reach these incarnate fiends, but if our friends of the North will punish them according to their desserts the South will be content."[232]

A Virginia newspaper reported on the "scenes in Boston" in detail and applauded their northern neighbors for defending the cause of slavery. "We predict, if the abolitionists do not succumb, that they will meet, at home, an awful punishment," the paper wrote.[233]

In Raleigh, North Carolina, the local newspaper could barely contain its glee upon learning the news of the abolitionists' comeuppance in Boston. "Even in the old Pilgrim city, Judge Lynch would not only open a court but…proceed to the infliction of summary justice on the culprit on his bar," it noted wryly.[234]

The rioting also caught the attention of the White House. President Andrew Jackson, who was in the final full year of his presidency and anxious to ensure a smooth transition to his chosen successor, Martin Van Buren, implicitly endorsed the mob's action. In remarks to Congress, Jackson made clear that he viewed the abolitionists as disloyal to the Union and applauded the good sense of northern states for rejecting their views. Without mentioning Thompson by name, the president singled out "emissaries from foreign parts" for interfering with the constitutional rights of the South. Rather than discouraging violence, Jackson seemed to indicate that if public expressions against abolitionists were not sufficient, they should take bolder steps to suppress "whatever is calculated to produce this evil."[235]

News of Boston's anti-abolitionist mob also rippled across the ocean, though the reaction in Great Britain and Ireland was far different. There, most saw the institution of slavery, rather than the abolitionist cause, as the greater evil. The British Parliament had already passed a series of antislavery measures culminating in the Slavery Abolition Act, which had gone into effect a little more than a year earlier. The contrasting political climate afforded the British press a more discerning perspective on the rising tide of abolitionist hostility in Boston and elsewhere. One progressive weekly newspaper in Manchester, England, summed it up aptly: "The rage against the abolitionists is not now confined to the Southern slaveholding states, but has extended itself to religious Boston, the nursery of American independence."[236] An Irish newspaper echoed this same view: "The inhabitants of the Eastern States seem anxious to conciliate their brethren of the Slave states."[237]

Sitting at his desk on the second floor of the Old State House, Mayor Lyman was faced with more provincial decisions. There had already been calls for him to call out the militia to preserve order, but he did not feel that necessary, nor did he believe he had the statutory authority to do so. Not to mention, many members of the militia were among those who had marched in the mob against the abolitionists, so the move may have been futile at best or incendiary at worst.

Some abolitionists and labor advocates also wanted the mayor to call a public meeting at Faneuil Hall so the outrages of this mob could be publicly denounced. The *Boston Reformer*, a newspaper proclaiming to be the voice of the working man, endorsed the move on free speech and civil liberty grounds, and the *Liberator* quickly agreed.[238] But Mayor Lyman had a different view.

Following a mob riot at a Catholic convent in Charlestown the previous summer, the mayor had chaired a meeting at Faneuil Hall with most of the city's leading citizens in attendance to condemn the shocking action. A series of resolutions was passed, and the attack on the building, "occupied only by defenseless females," was denounced in the sternest terms.[239] The mob's actions were viewed as an attack on the freedom of religion and a threat to law and order, and a citizen committee was established to investigate and bring the perpetrators to justice. The mayor's decisive actions were widely praised at the time, even though Charlestown was not even within the city limits.

But now, as he weighed the proper response to this mob, Lyman chose not to follow that same precedent. He did not see the two events as comparable. After all, the anti-Catholic rioters had torched the convent and burned it to the ground, but the anti-abolitionist rioters had caused little actual property damage. One was a premeditated attack, and the other was a mostly spontaneous and organic event. The anti-Catholic rioters threatened religious freedom and the cherished principles of liberty, while the abolitionists were just fanatics who threatened the sanctity of the Union. The convent mob was a rowdy and lawless crowd, composed of mostly laborers, sailors and unskilled workers—not his peers, the city's "gentlemen of property and standing."

How could they pose any real threat?

Chapter 17

LESSONS AND REUNIONS

What a collection of raving fanatics and dangerous incendiaries.

With mob activity subsiding, Susan Paul settled back into her duties as a seamstress, homemaker, and schoolteacher. Until recently, she likely taught classes on the ground floor of the African Meeting House, almost directly underneath the pulpit where her late father once preached. She was following in the footsteps of her mother, who began teaching primary school from the Paul family home on George Street a decade earlier.[240]

In March, the city opened its first stand-alone public school for Black children a few dozen steps from the church. The new African schoolhouse was formally dedicated in honor of Abiel Smith, a white businessman who bequeathed funds to the city for Black education. The Smith School House, as it was known, spanned three floors and could accommodate as many as two hundred students. An upper-floor grammar school taught subjects like spelling, writing, geography, arithmetic and bookkeeping, while the lower level served as a primary school for younger children and was where Paul probably taught, in addition to her ongoing Sunday school classes.[241]

With its handsome façade, gabled roof and brownstone windowsills, the new school was a marked improvement over the decrepit, confined and poorly ventilated space under the church. The unhealthy conditions there had contributed to poor student attendance, according to a Boston school committee report two years earlier, which labeled the situation "insidious and unjust."

The first public primary school for Black students in Boston opened at the African Meeting House in 1820. Today, the building is part of Boston's Museum of African American History. *MHS.*

In recommending that a new school be built, the committee offered a frank assessment of the current state of racial conditions: "If any distinction be made between [Black students], and others, it ought to be in their favour, and not against them; for their parents are precluded by custom and prejudice from those lucrative employments which enable whites to be liberal and public spirited."[242]

The new school, built at a cost of about $7,500, was formally opened on March 3, 1835, with remarks from William Minot, the school committee chairman. He spoke before a large crowd of mostly Black residents and students and shared a sanguine message: "The progress of truth is discouragingly slow in this world, but truth is not entirely stationary; it moves a little, and it is in our power to accelerate its course. The power in your hands is education."[243]

It was an uplifting message and a momentous day for all involved. For all the progressive sentiments, however, the new Smith School House remained officially segregated and lacked the same resources afforded the city's other public schools for white children.

Susan Paul took a keen interest in the success of her students and adopted a warm and encouraging teaching style, much like her mother. It proved a successful formula. Two years earlier, Garrison had visited her classroom with members of the New England Anti-Slavery Society and came back with a glowing report: her students were cheerful and readily completed their exercises, and Paul was a great credit to the school, they reported. "It is, however, her kindness which directs them, much more than force, to which we believe she seldom if ever resorts."[244]

Paul made it a point to teach her students more than just the traditional ABCs. She believed in using her schoolroom pulpit to introduce them to broader issues of racism and segregation, and her lessons came both in and out of the classroom. The previous summer, she took about thirty students for an afternoon event outside the city celebrating the abolition of slavery in the British colonies.

Paul's class included a handful of students who had been born enslaved, but most were from free Black families, and she wanted to make sure they also developed some understanding of the harsh realities of enslavement, as she made clear in her biography about young student James Jackson.

The antislavery hymns sung by her juvenile choir also served as a helpful learning tool, and Paul used them to great effect. Not only were their choir performances a popular attraction, delivering their antislavery message in song, but the lyrics also made useful texts to study reading and vocabulary. One tune performed by her juvenile choir focused on the issue of prejudice and articulated a powerful argument against the colonization movement. The lyrics delivered a message that was accessible to children but also had a relevance for all ages.

MR. PREJUDICE

Pray who is Mr. Prejudice,
We hear so much about,
Who wants to spoil our pleasant songs,
And keep the white folks out?

They say he runs along the streets,
And makes a shocking noise,
Scolding at little colored girls,
And whipping colored boys.

We never yet have met the wretch
Although our mothers say,
That colored folks, both old and young,
He torments every day.

A colonizing agent hired,
We're told he has a whip,
With which he flogs our honest friends,
And drives them to the ship.

The colonizers tell us all
They hate this wicked man—
Yet ask him every day to dine,
And flatter all they can.

He must be very tall and stout,
Quite dreadful in a rage,
For strongest colored men they say,
He'll toss out of a stage.

We wish that we could catch him here,
We think he'd hold his tongue,
If he should see our smiling looks,
And know how well we've sung.

However strong the rogue may be,
Kind friends, if you'll unite,
Should he peep in, oh, never fear,
We'll banish him to-night.[245]

Issues of race were not the only ones Paul incorporated into her lesson plans. She also taught her students temperance songs and core values of generosity, respect, and nonviolence.

The latter was certainly on the mind of her friend Garrison, a committed pacifist, who was making plans to leave Connecticut and return to the city. Garrison feared that any lengthy absence would be fodder for his critics and feed the false narrative that he'd been chased out of town for good. He also worried about the *Liberator*, which was now office-less and in a precarious financial condition.

"It seems to me that my presence in Boston is indispensable, on many accounts," he told a friend.[246]

On Wednesday morning, just two weeks after the mob attack, Garrison left the Brooklyn, Connecticut homestead with his father-in-law and rode to Providence, where he picked up the train to Boston. He traveled in one of the open carriage cars to save money and worried that he might be spotted along the way, but by the early evening, he was safely back in the city.

The plan was that his wife would stay behind in Connecticut with her parents, and he would divide his time between the two locales—at least until the baby was born and they could make a more permanent arrangement. Complicating matters was the fact that Garrison's landlord, a local grain merchant, demanded that he move out of the duplex he had rented on Brighton Street. He was fearful the growing anti-abolitionist and anti-Garrison sentiment would result in damage to his property.[247]

Instead of heading straight home upon his arrival, Garrison decided it would be better to have his coachman drop him off at a friend's house. With the recent rioting still fresh in his mind, he was apprehensive of who, or what, he might find waiting for him.

He found a welcome reception and a warm meal at the home of John Fuller. After tea, the men took a walk, initially in the direction of Garrison's home, until his friend let him in on a little secret: George Thompson was quietly staying nearby at the home of Joseph and Thankful Southwick. Garrison was eager to reunite with his old friend, and so the men proceeded to pay him a visit.

They found Thompson in "good health and spirits" and quickly caught up on the latest news and events. No sooner had the homecoming begun than it grew with the arrival of more abolitionist friends, including Charles Burleigh, Mary Parker and Mary Grew. "What a collection of raving fanatics and dangerous incendiaries," Garrison later described to his wife. "A happy meeting this!"[248]

After the joyful reunion, Garrison returned to his home on Brighton Street later that evening. There was no mob or burning effigy to greet him as he may have feared, just an unsigned note from an anonymous friend with a gift of forty-five dollars. The money, a pleasant and much-needed surprise, may have been from his friend John Vashon.

After a lengthy day of travel and reunion with his friends, an exhausted Garrison finally retired to his bed. His return to Boston had been more peaceful than his departure—at least so far. With his wife away in Connecticut, he had the bedroom to himself, so he allowed his beloved house cat to jump on the bed and purr away in her familiar spot. "We reposed very lovingly until morning, without any alarm from mobs without, or disturbance from rats within," he noted.[249]

Elsewhere in the city, Susan Paul was probably already in bed by that time, though with several young children and a crying baby in the home, her setting was certainly less tranquil than Garrison's.

When Susan's father died four and a half years earlier, the Paul family had been forced to move out of their home and now rented a modest dwelling down the street in the same North Slope neighborhood.[250] Her aged mother was still listed as the head of household in the city directory, but the responsibility for supporting the family was mostly borne by young Susan. Her late sister's husband was a talented musician but an absent father, and the bulk of childrearing fell to her.

When she wasn't in school, taking care of the children, leading her student choir or advancing the causes of social justice, she took on extra sewing work to make ends meet. Paul was not one to complain or ask others for help, but she did confide to close friends that she felt anxiety from time to time. Still, she remained driven by the antislavery cause; the burdens were many, but she knew the rewards were greater.

Chapter 18

EXIT THOMPSON

The most odious foreign renegade who ever visited this country.

Maria Chapman was already feeling the fallout from her outspoken abolitionist efforts. She had been shunned in certain social circles and did not even feel entirely comfortable at her own church. Recently, while standing by her front doorstep, three unidentified men had walked by and hissed at her.

Still, Chapman wanted to press the advantage in the wake of the mob attack and was eager to leverage her newfound notoriety to recruit more antislavery advocates. She was now pushing to have George Thompson travel to Weymouth to give a public lecture and help rally support in her hometown. Thompson was game, but most of the other abolitionists thought it too risky for him to venture out of his protective bubble. "The brethren seem horrified at the idea," Maria's sister wrote.[251]

Even a fortnight after the riot, the political climate in the city remained tense, and fears of further violence were on the minds of many abolitionists. It was felt that Thompson's reemergence or Garrison's return were both liable to set off a new surge of hostility.

"[Thompson] is hunted now like a wild beast," and Garrison is not safe in the city either, Anne Weston told her aunt. "The truth is that the abolitionists in Boston are not now under the protection of the laws," she warned.

As if to prove their point, a crowd of anti-abolitionists gathered and paraded down Washington Street with a band playing music. They carried a large hand-painted sign depicting George Thompson with the words "The

Phillips, Garrison and Thompson. *Yale University.*

Foreign Emissary" above his head. Next to him was drawn a Black woman asking, "When are we going to have another meeting, brother Thompson?" The menacing reference to the riot and the Boston Female Anti-Slavery Society meeting was obvious.

If the antipathy to her cause bothered Chapman, she did not show it. She persisted in her work despite the urgings from her sister and others to adopt a more cautious approach. "Maria has great enjoyments, I cannot say that I have," sister Anne wrote.

When it came to George Thompson, however, prudence prevailed, and plans were made for him to return to Great Britain. Thompson himself was reluctant to leave Boston but agreed it was for the best. "I believe many here were prepared to take [my life]—many more prepared to rejoice over the deed," he told a friend.[252]

Henry Chapman, who ran a ship chandler's business with his father, helped make the arrangements. Thompson would set sail for England, via New Brunswick, and his wife and children would first visit relatives and then join him later. Precautions were taken to keep the news quiet to prevent further disturbances.

Maria's sisters, especially Caroline, Anne and Deborah, had grown very fond of the eloquent Scotsman and were devastated to learn the news. Deborah was on her way to church when she first learned of his departure and ran home to tell her sisters. They all hurried over to Maria's house, where Henry Chapman advised them not to make a fuss with any final goodbyes "for fear of exciting suspicion."

It was a fruitless warning; they all decided to go anyway. Deborah and Caroline discreetly visited the Southwicks' home around eleven o'clock to make their goodbyes, and Anne came a short time later, staying until about noon, when it was time for Thompson to depart. A small party of abolitionists gathered to wish him off, including the recently returned Garrison. (He had decided to skip church that morning because he'd yet to replace his "Sunday Best" pants torn by the mob, and it was too warm to wear a cloak.)[253]

Henry Chapman brought Thompson down to Central Wharf in a horse carriage and then rowed him out to board a British sailing vessel, *Satisfaction*, recently arrived from England. By midnight, the brig had cleared the Massachusetts coastline and set sail toward St. John's, New Brunswick, ending George Thompson's fifteen-month odyssey in America.

His departure was a blow for the Boston abolitionist community. They were losing not only a devoted antislavery advocate but also a dear friend. Deborah Weston took it especially hard, calling it "a day of affliction" in her diary. Garrison was also saddened to see his friend depart; "the idea of separating from him—perhaps for the close of life—filled my soul with anguish," he confided to his wife.

Garrison recognized that his friend's premature farewell, spurred on by an anti-abolitionist mob, offered powerful editorial fodder to wield in the pages of the *Liberator*, and he fully embraced the opportunity. He viewed it as yet another indictment of Mayor Lyman's actions—or inactions—in failing to keep the peace of the city and protect the civil liberties of residents.

"He has gone! The paragon of modern eloquence—the benefactor of two nations—the universal philanthropist—the servant of God, and the friends of mankind—is no longer in our midst!" Garrison wrote in the pages of the *Liberator* with his customary dramatic flourish.[254]

Susan Paul was also disappointed to lose such a devoted ally to the antislavery cause. She penned a heartfelt letter to Thompson to thank him for his fidelity, zeal and perseverance as a "friend of the oppressed" and praised him for awakening the "sleeping energies of this guilty nation."[255]

Not everyone was disappointed, of course. Much of Boston was in fact quite pleased to see Thompson go—"the most odious foreign renegade who ever visited this country," said one commentator.[256] Threats against Thompson and Garrison also continued to pour in. One semi-coherent letter mailed to the *Liberator* promised violence if any future antislavery meetings were planned and pledged that this time "the mayor will not have a chance to save you from the tar kettle."[257]

The afternoon of Thompson's departure, Maria and Henry Chapman hosted Garrison in their home. There was much to catch up on, including some practical matters. Garrison, for one, needed a place to store all his furniture until he found a new place to live, so Maria's sister agreed to store it in her home. The Chapmans had already taken care of another loose end. The coachman who drove Garrison from the Old State House to the jail on the day of the riot had stopped by with a bill for fifty dollars for his services, which they were only too happy to pay given the bravery he'd shown.

The future of the *Liberator* may have also been part of the conversation. New subscribers continued to pour in, more than a dozen just on Monday, but the paper's financial situation was far from stable. Following its eviction from the publishing office, the newspaper's operations were moved to the antislavery office for the time being, but debts continued to pile up. (The antislavery office also became Garrison's temporary living quarters; several friends had offered to host him, but he preferred to sleep in the office on a sofa-bed.)

Garrison estimated that the business owed about $2,500 to creditors. Adding to the woes, his partner Isaac Knapp had formally decided to end their partnership and hereafter would just provide printing services.[258] Maria Chapman was eager to support the *Liberator*'s antislavery mission, and she and her husband may have quietly offered financial support. Garrison later hinted that he had arranged to settle his past accounts.

Monday also happened to be the date for state elections. Garrison eschewed politics and did not align himself with any party, but he couldn't help but take some pride in learning that he received write-in votes for a state legislative seat.[259]

While the antislavery cause was foremost in Maria Chapman's mind, she also had other worries, including her three-year-old-daughter Lizzie, who had recently contracted the measles. The city had faced an alarming influx of cases, and more than a dozen deaths were reported each week throughout the fall. Maria's younger sister agreed to stay over and help care for Lizzie.

There was no consensus as to why the outbreak occurred, and some debated whether the disease was infectious or not. A Boston medical journal weighed in on the topic with treatment guidance and acknowledged that there seemed to be in the city at the time "a peculiar condition of atmosphere favorable to its development."[260]

For abolitionists, Boston just did not seem to be a healthy place to be in any sense of the word.

Chapter 19

LOVE AND MARRIAGE

I am disgusted with this squeamish regard for Mr. Lyman.

If the cause had not yet stirred Wendell Phillips to action, there was one abolitionist who soon would. Ann Greene was a bright, outspoken and determined young woman with long hair and blue eyes just shy of her twenty-second birthday. She came from a wealthy Boston family, but her parents had both died when she was young, and she'd been raised by the family of her uncle, Henry Chapman (Maria Chapman's father-in-law).

Greene and her cousin Anna Grew had planned to ride out to her home in Greenfield, Massachusetts, a mill village about ninety miles west of Boston. Grew's fiancé, a promising young attorney named James Alvord, was to join the women for the lengthy carriage ride.[261] Alvord was eager to bring along a companion to entertain Ann Greene so that he could spend the time with his fiancée, so he asked a pair of young attorneys he knew to join him—Charles Sumner and Wendell Phillips.

On the morning they were to depart, Sumner begged off at the last moment, citing the unpleasant weather. He reportedly told Phillips that on such a day he wouldn't go on a stage ride with any woman, though his friend knew the decision probably had more to do with his shyness than the weather forecast.[262]

That left Phillips to serve the role of wingman alone. It would not be a simple task. Though in somewhat frail health, Ann Greene was not a young woman to be trifled with. She'd been described to Phillips as "the cleverest, loveliest, most brilliant young woman, but a rabid abolitionist. Look out or she will talk you into that *ism* before you suspect what she is about."[263] Greene was also a member of the Boston Female Anti-Slavery Society and had been inside the abolitionist office along with Maria Chapman, Susan Paul and others when the riot began.

Greene came as advertised and talked passionately of abolition for much of the long carriage ride. No doubt she had much to recount given her recent brush with the mob and her work with the women's antislavery society and William Lloyd Garrison. Phillips listened intently and was intrigued. He found her strong-willed and opinionated, though he could also see that she was warm-spirited and vivacious, and he certainly admired her passion. They both hailed from similar social circles, grew up in wealthy families and lost their fathers at a young age. When the ride was done, Phillips decided to ask if he could call on her again. She readily agreed.

Romance was probably not on the mind of Mayor Lyman. His successor had just been chosen during Monday's election, and his days in office were now coming to an end.[264] Lyman could have served another term as mayor if he wished, and in fact the Whig Party tried to renominate him, but he was ready to move on.

Lyman did not feel the criticism being leveled at him by the abolitionists was warranted—whether it was his handling of the mob or his tenure as mayor. He considered himself to be just as strong an antislavery man as anyone else, he told friends. After all, as mayor he had rebuffed requests from southern slave owners to capture and return enslaved persons who escaped to Boston, and he supported the establishment of the first public primary school for Black students in the city.[265] It seemed to him that the abolitionists wanted him to preserve law and order—except when that law conflicted with their own antislavery views.

The Boston press continued to support Lyman's view—save the *Liberator*, which persisted in its denunciations. A lengthy piece in the recent edition argued the case against the mayor in vigorous detail. The article, headed with the Latin phrase "Qui non vetat, cum debeat, et possit, Jubet" (he, whose duty it is to prevent wrong, and is able to prevent it, and does not, commands it), was signed by an abolitionist minister writing under the pen name "Hancock."[266]

The essay critiqued the mayor's actions dating back to the anti-abolitionist rally in August at Faneuil Hall and pointed out his purported misdeeds each step of the way. The interaction between Mayor Lyman and Maria Chapman and her fellow society members inside the lecture hall was replayed, though with some Garrisonian dramatic license.

The writer also took issue with the mayor's conduct since the mob. "Has he made any effort to redeem the honor of our disgraced city? Has he made any effort to detect and bring to condign punishment the authors of that scene of plunder and violence?"[267]

Lyman was not a regular reader of the *Liberator*, nor did the paper have much of a readership in his social circles, but he certainly took note of the article. His portrayal in the *Liberator* may not have been of paramount concern, but he did care about his legacy, and even some abolitionists felt the criticism was a bit harsh. One member of the New England Anti-Slavery Society, Reverend E.M.P. Wells, wrote to Garrison asking him to cancel his subscription after reading it.[268]

A defense of the mayor came in the next edition of the *Liberator* from an unlikely source: Samuel Sewall. Writing under the pen name "An Abolitionist," Sewall explained that he was "neither the eulogist, nor the apologist of Mr. Lyman" but felt that the earlier critique had gone too far.

"We should be just, even to our opponents," he wrote in refuting many of the charges against the mayor. Another rebuttal came the following week, and the back-and-forth debate would continue to linger on the pages of the *Liberator* for several more issues.

Garrison was irritated by the exchange and less willing to forgive and forget. "I am disgusted with this squeamish regard for Mr. Lyman, and think it very unwise, as well as positively criminal, for any to attempt to exonerate him from blame," he told a friend.[269]

Garrison had spent the past two weeks in Boston settling his affairs and trying to square away the *Liberator*. Over the weekend, in between the rainstorms, he moved out most of his furniture. Some of his belongings, including a sofa and rocking chair, he gave away to friends, while a few mementos were brought over to the antislavery office, including his prized portrait of the British antislavery leader Thomas Clarkson.[270] Perhaps just as important to Garrison was his beloved housecat, which he found a new home with Maria Chapman's sisters.

Now Garrison felt ready to return to Connecticut to be with his wife and her family. He'd made the mistake of citing his wife's "delicate" health among his reasons for originally leaving the city, in a column published the week prior in the *Liberator*. She was none too pleased and told him as much.[271] "When I see you, I will kiss you, and make it all up," he promised.

While Garrison made plans to leave the city once again, Maria Chapman, Susan Paul and the members of the Boston Female Anti-Slavery Society were making plans to finally finish their twice-interrupted and thrice-relocated annual meeting.

This time, they would attempt to hold the meeting in a less public setting and accepted an open invitation from Francis Jackson to host them in his home. Still, the women did not try to hide their intent. A notice was duly published in the *Liberator* several days ahead, stating that "punctual attendance is requested, as business of great importance is to come before the meeting."[272]

The day before the scheduled meeting was a busy one. George Thompson's wife was preparing to leave the city with her three children and eventually catch up to her husband. Garrison also shared the news that he would be taking the train back to Connecticut the next day. In the afternoon, Maria Chapman hosted her sisters for tea, and they chatted about plans for the society's meeting. A new visitor was expected to attend for the first time, Harriet Martineau, the British writer and reformer, who was on an extended tour of the United States.

The next morning, clouds gave way to sunshine. Chapman and her sister Ann had lunch with Martineau to make her acquaintance and then handle any last-minute arrangements for the meeting that afternoon. It was hoped that this foreign emissary would not engender the same hostility as the previous. Four weeks had passed since the mob riot, but anti-abolitionist sentiment remained strong.

By this point, Maria Chapman was ready for just about anything. Her sister Deborah summed up their collective attitude matter-of-factly, writing in her diary: "Busy all morning preparing to be mobbed."

Part II

1855

Austin criticized Lovejoy for provoking the mob incident and accused proponents of politicizing his death for their own cause. "I have little sympathy for a minister of the gospel who is found, gun in hand, fighting in a broil with a mob," he argued, declaring that Lovejoy had "died as the fool dieth."

Austin was a well-known figure in the city and one of the state's leading law enforcement officers, and many found his remarks compelling. The raucous crowd reacted with a tense mix of hisses and applause. Some spectators feared that the resolutions could be voted down.

The din of the hall eventually abated when a young man—a stranger to most—strode forward unannounced and stepped onto the raised platform. His voice quickly commanded the attention of the cavernous hall. Wendell Phillips did not have formal remarks prepared and could not have predicted the curveball Austin had just thrown, but his antislavery feelings had been percolating and germinating for some time. His moment had arrived.

Phillips gestured to the historic portraits hanging on the wall inside Faneuil Hall and launched into a stinging rebuke of Austin. "Sir, when I heard the gentleman lay down principles which place the murderers of Alton side by side with Otis and Hancock, with Quincy and Adams, I thought those pictured lips would have broken into voice to rebuke the recreant American—the slanderer of the dead."

There was a thunderclap of approval, mixed in with boisterous shouts, jeers and hisses. "Take that back!" came the cry from some. Two men rose and marched toward the platform on either side of Phillips. Thinking they intended to put an end to Phillips's speech, the Austin contingent reacted with glee, shouting out, "He shan't go on till he takes it back"—until it became apparent the two men meant to protect Phillips to ensure he could finish his remarks.

"Fellow-citizens, I cannot take back my words," Phillips countered calmly. "Surely the Attorney-General, so long and well known here, needs not the aid of your hisses against one so young as I am,—my voice never before heard within these walls!"

The crowd settled down, and Phillips continued with his speech for at least twenty-five more minutes. He first laid out the facts of the case in lawyerly fashion, deconstructing and dismantling the attorney general's arguments, and then drew comparisons to the Patriots of the Revolutionary War defending the rights of free speech.

By the time Phillips wound down his remarks, the passage of the Lovejoy resolutions seemed a foregone conclusion. His soaring eloquence and powerful oratory had won over the crowd. When it came time to vote, the measures won overwhelming support, and many of Austin's backers, now resigned to the outcome, did not even bother to cast a vote.

The immediate reaction to Phillips's speech was highly favorable, and as years passed, it took on even greater significance in abolitionist lore. "I think Mr. Phillips' power over that audience was one of the most remarkable scenes on record,"[283] recalled Sarah Southwick, who had sat near Maria Chapman in the gallery. Others referred to it as "the birth speech of Wendell Phillips." Many years later, the *Boston Globe* called it "one of the most memorable and effective appeals for freedom that has ever waked the echoes of the old Faneuil Hall."[284]

Now, as the twentieth anniversary of the Gentlemen's Mob approached, Boston abolitionists decided it would be a fitting time for a celebration of sorts. "It will be a favorable time to contrast the Anti-Slavery of 1835 with the Anti-Slavery of 1855," one suggested.[285] Naturally, they would hold the event at the same location from which the Boston Female Anti-Slavery Society had been expelled. The lecture room, known as Stacy Hall, could accommodate up to four hundred people, and tickets were sold for fifteen cents each. The speakers included Garrison, Edmund Quincy and Theodore Parker, but Phillips was listed first.

At twenty-three years old, Phillips was a curious spectator in broadcloth; at twenty-six, an impressive and eloquent newcomer; and now, at forty-three years of age, with speckles of gray in his sweeping sideburns, Phillips had become a leading abolitionist voice. The young man who had never met William Lloyd Garrison or even picked up his radical newspaper was now the namesake for his third son and served on the *Liberator*'s finance committee.[286]

It was a windy, rain-soaked Sunday afternoon in October—a far cry from the unseasonably warm and pleasant weather two decades earlier. The contrast had not escaped Garrison's notice. "The storm of today is of the Lord—it is well; the storm twenty years ago was of the Adversary—it was ill," he remarked.

An enthusiastic crowd flowed into the building, filling up Stacy Hall and spilling into the hallways, but there were no incendiary handbills or angry hecklers, and the city's mayor, Jerome V.C. Smith—a rather unconventional politician who had his own experience with mobs—hardly took notice.[287] The meeting got underway at 2:30 p.m. with sixty-six-year-old Francis Jackson presiding in what was assumed to be his final curtain call.[288]

After introductions, Garrison took the podium and spoke for over an hour, first reciting the early history of the abolition movement and then

EPILOGUE

Susan Paul

Susan Paul did not live to hear Wendell Phillips's stirring words on the twentieth anniversary of the Gentlemen's Mob. After a hiatus, Paul resumed her popular student choir performances in February 1837 with an event at Congress Hall. Tickets were twenty-five cents. Additional performances were held in early May at the antislavery office, in June at a Boston meetinghouse and on the Fourth of July in the nearby city of Lynn, accompanying a lecture by newcomer Wendell Phillips.

The students and their teacher impressed on every occasion. "We sat in our place, absolutely enchanted. Tears flowed on every side; and the audience gave vent to their enthusiastic admiration, by long and reiterated bursts of applause," one reviewer wrote.[293]

As before, Paul made sure her talented students were not just singing all the right melodies but also hitting the appropriate political notes. Her concerts mixed classical and religious tunes with songs that conveyed important messages, like "Mr. Prejudice," pointing out the hypocrisy of the colonization movement; "The Sugar Plums," decrying the use of southern slave labor; and "Strike the Cymbal," a rallying cry for freedom.

Paul remained active as an officer in the Anti-Slavery Society and served as a delegate for the women's national antislavery convention, first held in 1837 in New York and again the following year in Philadelphia. She was

Susan Paul is depicted in the *Anti-Slavery Almanac* sharing a lesson with a student about a stolen apple to make a point about the evils of slavery. *From the* Anti-Slavery Almanac, *1837*.

among a small number of Black women who participated and was also selected to serve as an officer for at least one of the conventions.

While most of the white women who were active in the antislavery movement hailed from affluent, or at least middle-class, families, Paul teetered on the brink of insolvency after the deaths of her father and sister forced her into the role of family breadwinner. Her younger brother, Thomas Paul Jr., was on his way to a successful career as an educator (and would later become one of the first Black graduates of Dartmouth College), but he was not able to contribute much to the family during this period, and so Susan Paul was left to carry the burden. The modest proceeds from the sale of her book may have helped, along with her teaching and seamstress income, but it wasn't always enough.

Financial pressures forced the Paul family to move several times, and in 1837, they rented a home on Grove Street in the same North Slope section of Beacon Hill. They intended to split the $200 annual rent with another Black resident, but the plan fell through, and Paul was forced to do something she loathed, which was ask for financial help. She reached out to her fellow abolitionists to share her struggles to care for her family and cover the rent.

Lydia Maria Child promptly took up her cause and wrote letters on her behalf. "Miss Paul is high-spirited, and I believe suffered much before she complained. Day before yesterday, she sent for me, and told me her distress, and how she struggled with it, rather than make it known to the abolitionists, who were called to sacrifice so much for the colored people," Child wrote asking for donations on her behalf. Jonathan Phillips, a relative of Wendell Phillips, promptly wrote back to Child with a contribution of thirty dollars.[294]

Paul remained loyal to Garrison even as Boston's growing abolitionist movement began to splinter toward the end of the decade. A bitter struggle ensued within the Boston Female Anti-Slavery Society, with Maria Chapman and her sisters advocating for a broader, bolder, progressive agenda, while others, including society president Mary Parker and Martha Ball, preferred a conservative approach and felt the group should stick to its core antislavery mission. Religious and class divisions also fed into the competing factions, and support for the iconoclastic Garrison became a flash point.[295]

Paul sided with the Chapman camp, though she was no doubt displeased to see the infighting tear the society asunder. She had never been shy about speaking out for the cause of freedom, but she was known to be amiable and kind-hearted and did not appear drawn to conflict in the same way as Chapman.

In early 1840, Paul faced her own personal challenge with the unexpected death of her fiancé. Little is known about the man, but he may have died from tuberculosis. He and Paul had been expected to be married soon.

Later that same year, near the five-year anniversary of the Gentlemen's Mob, Paul took a steamboat to visit New York City, probably for a meeting of the American Anti-Slavery Society. As a Black woman, she was not allowed to stay in the women's cabin, so she slept on the lower deck instead. A blast of cold air and rain descended, and Paul was left to brave the elements overnight. As a result, she later developed a bronchial infection.[296]

The lingering illness did not keep her from working at the annual antislavery fair held later in December. Paul manned a table selling a variety of linens, crafts and handmade goods to raise money. She sat near Chapman in front of a large ornamental vase on a white marble slab decorated with fresh holiday greens. Antislavery slogans hung from the tables and walls, and a plaster bust of Garrison perched on a pedestal stood in the middle of the room. Tea was served along with jellies and maple sugar candies, and Christmas melodies filled the air. Any divisions were temporarily cast aside; it was a festive and joyful occasion, one that Paul had always enjoyed in the past.

This year, however, her poor health got the better of her, and Paul had to leave early. She was confined to bedrest and unable to attend the Christmas soiree on the final night to cap off the successful event.

Her friends tried to comfort her, but she never recovered. Four months later, Susan Paul died at the age of thirty-one. Services were held in her father's old church, and she was buried in South Boston. "The family will now be broken up and the children taken by sundry friends,"[297] Maria Chapman's sister explained in breaking the news. Sarah Southwick later recalled how her death was another example of the "cruelty of this prejudice."[298]

Paul's efforts at her final society fair raised twenty dollars for the antislavery cause.[299]

Theodore Lyman

Had he still been alive, it's unlikely that **Theodore Lyman** would have attended the twentieth anniversary of the Gentlemen's Mob. Once his mayoral term ended, Lyman stepped out of the limelight and largely stayed there, preferring to focus his energies on gardening and philanthropic causes. His frequent charitable acts included generous donations to the Boston Seamen's Aid Society, Boston Lying-in Hospital, Fatherless and Widows Society and the Massachusetts Horticultural Association.

Lyman's wife, Mary, died in the summer of 1836, followed two years later by his father, Theodore Lyman Sr. (One New York newspaper incorrectly reported the death of the younger Lyman—a "typographical homicide" that was quickly pounced on by the Boston press.)[300] The expansive gardens and exotic flowers Lyman had cultivated reminded him too much of his late wife, so he later moved to nearby Brookline. His family estate, known as the Vale, remains in Waltham, Massachusetts, and features one of the nation's oldest greenhouses.

Lyman took ill in 1849 while traveling with his son in Europe. He returned home in the summer and died a short time later at the age of fifty-seven. His

The Lyman fountain in Dorchester, circa 1885. *HathiTrust*.

will included a generous bequest of $50,000 to support a reform school for juvenile offenders.[301]

Boston civic leaders later recognized Lyman's efforts to deliver fresh water to the city by dedicating a public water fountain in his honor in 1885. The dedication ceremony, held in the Dorchester neighborhood of Boston, featured a parade of prominent speakers who extolled Lyman's virtues. Several referenced his actions during the Gentlemen's Mob, praising him as a "courageous man" who took a "bold and fearless stand" against the mob and who "twice or thrice rescued [Garrison], almost single-handed, and saved his city from indelible disgrace."[302]

JAMES HOMER

James L. Homer, the *Boston Commercial Gazette* editor and anti-abolitionist agitator, later confessed his regret for the role he played in instigating the Gentlemen's Mob. His hopes of profiting off southern proslavery business interests had not panned out, and the man who was once among the city's most prominent residents and served as a member of the state legislature later saw his fortunes take a turn for the worse. One of his former apprentices later recalled seeing Homer and barely recognizing his old boss. He appeared "a dirty and dissipated-looking object, face swelled up with beer drinking, shoes broken, clothes ragged, and in every way a journeyman tramp."[303]

Homer found work for a time in the composing room of a Boston print shop that happened to be in the same spot as the former antislavery office. His former apprentice could not resist commenting on the irony. "Homer, this is the room you and your mob drove Mr. Garrison from, and you are now standing barefoot upon the very identical spot where Mr. Garrison's desk stood," he recalled. Homer lasted for a time in Boston and later moved to Baltimore, where he reportedly died in jail.[304]

"BUFF" COOLEY

Aaron "Buff" Cooley, the burly truckman who helped Garrison, also had his ups and downs. He later got married and worked at a hotel and saloon. At one point, he served as a landlord for tenement buildings in the city and got in hot water for allowing one of them to be used as a brothel. Eventually, he opened his own lodging house, a popular spot called the Half-Way House that was known for its boiled clams and fish chowder.

Cooley ran into hard times later in life, and after learning that abolitionists had contributed funds to help Garrison and his lifetime of antislavery work, Cooley decided to try and capitalize on his brush with history by asking for money too. He continued his letter writing campaign for many years, with some success. "If you can make it convenient to draw me one hundred and fifty dollars I want to go to Washington D.C. and have not got a dollar to do anything with," he wrote to Garrison in 1868, pledging that "this will be my last letter to you."[305] It was not.

"Buff" was still well known and liked around the city, and the *Boston Daily Advertiser* even took up the cause on the thirty-fourth anniversary of the Gentlemen's Mob in 1869 with a public appeal, calling him "a West End boy of undaunted courage" whose service had not been properly recognized. He was now "a poor man, well advanced in years," with a family in need, the paper wrote.[306]

Cooley's persistent efforts worked, to a degree, and several of Garrison's friends did send him money. Initially, Garrison was receptive to Cooley's plight and wrote a polite letter in 1859 thanking him for any role he played in his rescue from the mob. But the incessant fundraising appeals eventually drew Garrison's ire, and he penned what amounted to a cease-and-desist letter in 1868.

But Cooley did not give up and reportedly accosted Garrison outside his home in 1871 with another demand for money. When that was not successful, he threated a libel lawsuit against Garrison. The endless appeals finally ended when Cooley died in 1872 at the age of sixty-two. Garrison's son later quipped that there would soon be a new demand coming "to support his widow to the remainder of her days."[307]

JOHN VASHON

From his home in Pittsburgh, **John B. Vashon** continued to support the *Liberator* and his friend Garrison. His popular barbershop remained a focal point of the antislavery movement in the city, and Vashon served in a variety of leadership roles for the abolitionist cause. Vashon's public bathhouse became a key pitstop for enslaved persons escaping from the South on the

Underground Railroad, and he also led efforts to improve access to public education for Black students in the city.

Vashon continued to serve as a subscription agent for the *Liberator*, and he and Garrison continued their regular correspondence. In the summer of 1847, Garrison wrote to tell Vashon he would be visiting Pennsylvania along with Frederick Douglass for a lecture tour. In his letter, he took the opportunity to reminisce about the Gentlemen's Mob and Vashon's visit to him at the jail that evening, noting his friend's kindness in bringing him a new fur hat.

"How many important events have transpired since that time, all deeply affecting our glorious anti-slavery cause! What battles have been fought, what victories won, by the uncompromising and undaunted friends of emancipation!" Garrison wrote.[308]

Vashon's benevolence and social justice advocacy were well known, but he was also a talented businessman, and he amassed a small fortune during his lifetime. Sadly, Vashon did not live to see the fruits of his emancipation labors. He died from a heart attack in 1854 while sitting in a train station in Pittsburgh waiting to get on a train to Philadelphia for a national convention for veterans of the War of 1812.

Vashon's life was celebrated in the pages of the *Liberator*. He had led a "brave and honorable" life, and his kindness, generosity and dedication to advancing the rights of Black citizens were unparalleled, the paper noted. His son, George B. Vashon, carried forth his mantel as a prominent antislavery advocate and later had a distinguished career as a law professor. He married Susan P. Vashon, the niece of Susan Paul.

MARTHA BALL

Like Maria Chapman, **Martha V. Ball** was joined in her antislavery work by her sisters, in her case Lucy and Hannah. Unlike Chapman, Ball did not embrace all the same progressive abolition principles as Garrison. When the Boston Female Anti-Slavery Society splintered into two factions, Ball and her sisters sided with Mary Parker and formed a competing Female Emancipation Society. Chapman did not take it well and once wrote, "This was war, to the knife's point." Ball remained active in her antislavery work for many years and later began working with a women's moral reform society, where she published an affiliated newspaper and several books. Ball lived into her eighties and was one of the oldest survivors of the Gentlemen's Mob. She died in December 1894.

LAVINIA HILTON

Lavinia Hilton remained an active member of the Boston Female Anti-Slavery Society and sided with the Chapman faction during the split. She regularly contributed to the annual antislavery fair, served with Susan Paul in a Black women's temperance society and joined an effort to repeal a state law prohibiting interracial marriage. Occasionally, she even performed along with Susan Paul in a singing group. Hilton's husband, John, a successful barber and businessman, was equally active. He was a close friend of Garrison's, a leader in the national antislavery movement and served as grand master of a Masons Hall. Lavinia Hilton died in November 1882.

WENDELL PHILLIPS

In the years marching up to the Civil War, **Wendell Phillips** continued his antislavery campaign with unmatched zeal, intellect and eloquence, earning the moniker of abolition's "golden trumpet"—or, as one critic declared him, an "infernal machine set to music."[309]

A southern slaveholder inadvertently illustrated his appeal: "I have been to hear Wendell Phillips speak, and such words, such abuse...the rascal deserves to be hung," the man complained. When asked why, if he was so offended, he had sat through Phillips's lengthy, hour-long remarks, he responded, "Confound the fellow, I couldn't get away from him."[310]

The legend of Phillips's celebrated oratory spread quickly. His frequent lectures, public speeches and "abolitionizing trips," paired with his fierce views on disunionism, racial equality, and social reform, had earned him a national audience on par with Garrison and Frederick Douglass.

It also earned him plenty of enemies. Threats, acts of violence and mobs were now a reoccurring feature wherever he spoke. Phillips thrived before antagonistic audiences but did still fear for his safety, and at one point, he began to carry a revolver and surround himself with bodyguards for protection.

"His precious life is in very great danger....We are quite sure of a mobocratic outbreak," Garrison wrote of his friend after learning of a plot against him, and this time at least the worry was not mere hyperbole. Another memorable message was delivered via package to the Phillips home. **Ann Greene Phillips** saw the unusual square box, neatly packed, and at first feared it might be detonating powder. Her adopted daughter, Phoebe, carefully opened the lid and peaked in, where she found a dead tabby cat coiled up inside. "There lay the poor dear fellow creature…cold and breathless!"[311]

Behind the scenes, Ann continued to play a pivotal role in her husband's work as trusted counsel and advocate, occasionally nudging him when she felt it necessary—this despite the constant health woes that kept her secluded and often confined to bed. She also kept up a regular correspondence with Maria Chapman and the Weston sisters, as well as Garrison and other leading abolitionists, and did not shy from dispensing her advice on political matters.

As the Civil War began, Wendell Phillips remained skeptical of Abraham Lincoln, once referring to him as "the slave-hound of Illinois."[312] Even after the Emancipation Proclamation, he worried that the president was too much of a compromiser, too ready to sacrifice his principles for a "sham peace." Phillips broke with Garrison in opposing Lincoln's reelection in 1864 and proposed a formal resolution at the state antislavery convention denouncing the president's actions. Garrison, for once, preferred a more diplomatic approach and tried to amend the resolution with softer language.

In this case, Phillips's hardline views prevailed. He may have been a slower convert to the abolitionist cause, but his views were at least as uncompromising as Garrison's—and now perhaps more. Critics pounced, claiming a "schism in the Abolition Church,"[313] though Garrison was quick to downplay any division.

The episode did portend a divergence in tactics, if not strategy. After the war, and the passage of the Thirteenth Amendment in Congress to abolish slavery, Garrison stepped back into semi-retirement. "My vocation, as an Abolitionist, thank God, has ended,"[314] he told the American Anti-Slavery Society in the spring of 1865.

Phillips, on the other hand, seemed to be getting his second wind. He objected to Garrison's push to dissolve the society and instead took over as president, staking out absolutist positions on Black enfranchisement and Reconstruction that were sometimes at odds with his old friend. The tension continued into the following year, even after Garrison reached out with a conciliatory letter stressing their shared views.[315]

The hoped-for reset of their relationship did not go as planned. Dissension at another meeting of the Massachusetts Anti-Slavery Society, followed by a spate of pointed letters in the press, dragged the breach further out into the public eye. Garrison, who had recently published his final issue of

Wendell Phillips, circa 1865–80. *LOC.*

the *Liberator*, continued to believe that the apparatuses of the antislavery movement were "happily obsolete" and preferred to focus on other ways of supporting newly freed Black people.

Phillips saw things differently. Abolishing slavery was not merely ending the practice of human chattel, he felt; "the object was to put the negro on an equality with the white race."[316] He believed that universal male suffrage should be a pre-condition before any southern state be readmitted to the Union and continued to press for strong-worded resolutions against anything less. "The Rebellion has not ceased. It has only changed its weapons," he announced.[317]

What finally helped thaw the ice between the two men was a blast from the past—the publication of a pamphlet by Mayor Lyman's son in 1870 relitigating his father's role in the Gentlemen's Mob. Both Garrison and Phillips took great offense and joined in correspondence to discredit the effort. Sharing a common agenda and foe—in this case, Lyman's son— may have been therapeutic to their strained friendship. Eventually, the two men would patch up their differences, and Phillips prominently eulogized Garrison's wife at her funeral, and later Garrison himself, following his death in 1879.

Phillips never took his eye off his life's mission against racial discrimination, but he poured his energies into a range of social reforms, including temperance, fair labor practices, women's rights, the plight of Native Americans, penal reform and the exploitation of Chinese immigrants. "We sheathe no sword. We only turn the front of the army upon a new foe," he declared in 1870 at the final meeting of the American Anti-Slavery Society following passage of the Fifteenth Amendment.[318]

The inherent conflict between labor and capital was a recurring theme in his work, and Phillips left no doubt that he came down on the side of the worker. Many of his arguments would resonate more than a century later in contemporary political discourse. He advocated for an eight-hour workday and currency reform, railed against the influence of "moneyed corporations" in the political process and decried what he saw as growing income inequality in the nation.

"This system of finance by which one man at sixty years old has gathered fifty millions of dollars, and of the ten thousand men that work for him, seven thousand get up every morning not knowing where dinner is coming from—that system of finance belongs to the bottomless pit, and the sooner it goes home the better," Phillips declared during a speech in Newburyport, Massachusetts, in the fall of 1871. "For, gentlemen, the great danger that threatens us in the future is the money power."[319]

Phillips's later years were not all filled with glory and accolades. A lifetime driven by pursuit of social reform, rather than financial gain, eventually depleted his savings and left him struggling to pay his debts, while he continued to care for Ann, who was now partially paralyzed. A far worse indignation came courtesy of his native city of Boston, which, beginning in 1880, commenced plans to demolish the Phillipses' home on Essex Street to pave the way for a street expansion. After unsuccessful appeals and delays, the Phillipses were eventually forced to decamp their home of four-plus decades to make way for an expanded Harrison Avenue. The march of commerce and business interests that Phillips had railed against for so long had claimed another victim.

One of Phillips's last public acts was to speak at the dedication of a statue of Harriet Martineau in Boston in December 1883. In his remarks, he referenced her passing through the city on the same day as the Gentlemen's Mob. "She came here to gain a personal knowledge of the Abolitionists, and her first experience was with the mob on State Street," he recalled. Though he was now in his early seventies with silvery hair, Phillips's voice remained strong, and he appeared still vibrant. The

Phillips stands in the doorway of his home on Essex Street, which was torn down to make way for a street expansion in 1882. *BPL.*

assembled crowd could not have known that it would be the final public speech of his remarkable career.

The following month, Phillips began to experience chest pains. His doctors prescribed various remedies, but the pains persisted and spread. He remained in bed in a weakened state for most of January. After a night taking mutton broth and beef tea, Phillips temporarily felt better, but the pain soon returned. On the afternoon of Saturday, February 2, 1884, he fainted while trying to lift himself out of bed. "I'm dying," he told his doctor, speaking truth to the end.

For Wendell Phillips, his manner of death came in marked contrast to his manner of life: calmly, quietly and without struggle, "as if he was just going to sleep," his doctor said.[320]

News of Phillips's death soon carried in newspapers across the nation. A public memorial was held at Faneuil Hall, and the sidewalks overflowed with mourners. Tributes poured in from pulpits, political leaders, and newspapers across the country. The *Boston Globe* published a full page of memorials from leading citizens, including Frederick Douglass, Julia Ward Howe, Lewis Hayden, Henry Ward Beecher and Lucy Stone.

"In his death New England has lost its most eloquent orator and its most courageous and brilliant reformer," wrote Douglass. He was one of the nation's "most daring and uncompromising leaders," added Howe.

The Massachusetts State Senate interrupted an afternoon session for members to offer their own words of praise. "Phillips belonged to the small class of men who can be called both great and good," said one state senator. Another called him the "apostle of equal rights."[321]

Prominent African American newspapers also sounded off. Lucretia Newman Coleman, a Canadian-born writer whose father escaped enslavement, penned a poetic tribute to Phillips in the *Christian Recorder* that referenced his early experiences with mobs and praised him for displaying that "rarest type of bravery." She wrote of Phillips, "Thou canst say of negro slavery, 'I sat by its cradle, I lived under its roof, I administered its bane, I followed its hearse, I shouted o'er its grave.'"[322]

Some eulogists noted the role of the Gentlemen's Mob in Phillips's conversion to the cause. As a young man watching the "merciless mob" drag Garrison through the streets of Boston in 1835, "his pure soul was stirred within him," one minister recounted. "At once he became the champion of the oppressed colored men of his own native land."[323]

In April, another public memorial service was held at the Tremont Temple, and Archibald Grimké, a prominent author and attorney who had grown up in enslavement in South Carolina, delivered a stirring eulogy. He retold Phillips's transformation from Puritan patrician attorney to antislavery agitator, recalling the day that free speech and the freedom of the press were dragged through the streets by the Gentlemen's Mob. Phillips had watched as only Maria Chapman and the other brave women had stood up for liberty on that day, Grimké told the crowd.

Frederick Douglass. *National Archives.*

"His eyes thus anointed, he began to see things as they were."[324]

Grimké sang the praises of Garrison and Charles Sumner but maintained that "tonight we are standing by the open grave of the greatest of the three."

Ann Greene Phillips, despite her lengthy and debilitating illness, outlived her husband for another fourteen months. Her passing came with far less fanfare, though she probably deserved the most credit for influencing her husband's chosen vocation. If the Gentlemen's Mob had planted the seed, she had certainly provided its sustenance. It's hard to imagine that the man once described as the "proud leader of the aristocracy" would have grown into the nation's preeminent social crusader without her impact.

Maria Chapman

Maria Weston Chapman did not attend the twentieth anniversary of the Gentlemen's Mob because she was living in Europe. The years sandwiched in between had been eventful.

In the months immediately after the riot, Chapman poured her energies into her abolitionist work with increasing vigor. She took over management of the annual antislavery fair, eventually growing it into a major fundraising vehicle, and penned the society's widely read annual report "Right and Wrong in Boston." The following summer, she published an antislavery song book, *Songs of the Free*, filled with popular hymns and religious songs from mostly female authors.[325]

Later, she began publishing her own antislavery literary gift book, called *The Liberty Bell*, which featured original poetry, letters and prose

Maria Chapman, circa 1846.
Boston Athenaeum.

from a variety of abolitionist writers. The first edition, some two hundred pages, was published in December 1839 and priced at fifty cents a copy, with proceeds benefiting the Massachusetts Anti-Slavery Society.

Chapman's involvement with the *Liberator* also grew. She assisted with editing and publishing duties and frequently contributed her own articles and poetry, typically using her initials as a byline. (Garrison referred to her as "our well-known correspondent M.W.C.") In time, she would become Garrison's key lieutenant or, as one critic later described her, "Garrison's evil genius." Others would later refer to her as "Captain Chapman" or "Joan of our Arc."[326]

She also had two more children during this time, Ann and Gertrude, who joined older siblings Lizzie and Henry Jr. The latter was, by all accounts, a handful, and Maria's sisters griped about his poor behavior.

A new decade ushered in a challenging period for the family. Her husband, Henry, took ill with tuberculosis and required a great deal of nursing and attention. "He is looking better and getting stronger but living with him gives one the settled idea that he is a short-lived man," Maria's sister wrote in the fall of 1840.[327] The following spring, young Gertrude died at ten months from unknown causes, possibly tuberculosis.[328] To treat Henry's debilitating illness, the couple traveled to the West Indies in the hopes that the warmer climate would help reduce his coughing fits, sweats, and muscle aches. Despite some periods of improvement, his condition deteriorated over time.

Chapman had her own personal health challenges to overcome as well. After speaking at a women's antislavery convention in Philadelphia in 1838, she developed a "brain fever," according to her physician. The diagnosis came following an incident at the convention when a violent proslavery mob interrupted the speeches with a barrage of rocks thrown against the windows. Their actions caused a deafening noise, and there was genuine fear inside the hall among the delegates. Chapman herself reportedly collapsed and may have suffered an anxiety attack. (The women had good reason to be fearful. The next night, the mob returned and burned down the hall.) Garrison also attended the convention and witnessed the incident. He feared the worst for his friend and shared the news with characteristic melodrama.

"Probably by the time this reaches you, she will be no more," he wrote a relative a week later. "There is no hope of her recovery."[329]

When she finally made it home, Chapman's doctor applied leeches and cut her hair to relieve her suffering. After a period of bedrest, her sister reported that she seemed to improve. "Her mind appears to dwell less on exciting events and abstract questions," she wrote.[330] Still, rumors of Chapman's "madness" abounded, some rooted in misogynistic attitudes about the role of women in political matters and others in old-fashioned gossip. Her family worked to manage her health as well as her reputation. One friend advised them not to heed all the misrepresentations. "This world babble is of little consequence," she wrote.[331]

Chapman recovered later that year, but her husband's declining health and need for constant care rekindled anxieties. She juggled it all with her own motherhood duties and her continued antislavery efforts. In the fall of 1842, Henry Chapman finally succumbed to his illness. His funeral was held on October 6, the day that would have been the couple's twelfth wedding anniversary. Fulfilling one of his final wishes, Maria donated fifty dollars in his name to help sustain the *Liberator*.[332]

By this time, Chapman was financially secure, though widowhood presented its own set of challenges. To further her children's education and escape the confines of Boston, Chapman decided to move to Europe for a spell. It would give her a fresh start and allow her to continue her abolitionist efforts in a new venue. In the summer of 1848, she set sail with her three children and sister Caroline, and after a short tour in Great Britain, they settled in Paris. Other Weston family members later joined them.

Chapman's European tour allowed her to reconnect with abolitionist friends abroad, including George Thompson and Harriet Martineau, and expand her antislavery circle of influence. Leveraging abolitionist support abroad was viewed as critical to the movement's broader domestic goals.

Chapman traveled extensively to continue her antislavery work, including visits to Germany, Italy, Switzerland and, frequently, Great Britain. She remained active in her writing, sending back regular contributions for the *Liberator* and *The Liberty Bell*, and hosted visitors from across the pond, including Harriet Beecher Stowe, whose influential new novel *Uncle Tom's Cabin* vividly depicted the harsh conditions for enslaved Americans and was already causing quite a buzz. Chapman also spent time getting to know the French writer and historian Alexis de Tocqueville.

What was initially intended to be a two- or three-year sojourn had stretched to seven by the time Chapman finally prepared to return home in the fall of 1855. Her daughter Lizzie, now married to a Frenchman, would remain in Paris along with some other family members.

By all accounts, Chapman considered her tour abroad a success. She had given her children a proper "finishing" education, successfully married off one daughter and seemingly straightened out her headstrong son. She had forged new friendships and connections and kept the pace with a full plate of abolitionist work, all while promoting the Garrison brand of immediate emancipation. Her new friends were saddened at her departure.

"God grant that in seeing your country again you will find there, new consolations, new encouragement, to preserve in the great cause which you have adopted as the main goal of your life," wrote Nicholas Tourgueneff, an exiled Russian noble living in France, who became a Garrisonian abolitionist convert.[333]

Chapman returned to her hometown of Weymouth, Massachusetts, in November 1855 to the news that her father, Warren, had died at age seventy-five. His death was not unexpected but was still an emotional blow.

She was warmly welcomed back by her abolitionist family. Garrison was particularly effusive in praising her efforts abroad and heralding her triumphant return. "It will be almost like a resurrection from the dead, or a return from a higher plan of spiritual existence," he wrote.[334] He also shared the news of the recent twentieth-anniversary celebration at Stacy Hall ("a most thrilling occasion…full of heart stirring reminisces")[335] and lamented that she had not returned in time to attend.

Chapman wasted no time in diving back into her abolition work, organizing the new antislavery bazaar in December, which remained the abolitionists' key fundraising vehicle, and publishing another tract, *How Can I Help to Abolish Slavery?* geared to new antislavery converts. She continued to publish *The Liberty Bell*, serve as officer of the Massachusetts Anti-Slavery Society and contribute to the *Liberator*. "She could keep more irons in the fire without burning one of them, than any person I ever knew," one friend later recalled.[336]

The next five years were a tumultuous time for the abolition movement—and the nation. A series of events pushed the nation closer to the disunion Garrison now advocated, including the crisis in Kansas, the Supreme Court's *Dred Scott* decision, the rise of militant antislavery movements and the raid on Harpers Ferry, and the emergence of a new antislavery Republican Party. The violent attack on their friend U.S. senator Charles Sumner by a proslavery congressman from South Carolina also hit close to home.

The final edition of the *Liberator* was published on December 29, 1865. *Dyer Memorial Library.*

$200 to Garrison to help cover the cost. In an emotional letter of thanks, Garrison reflected on their nearly three decades of work together. He felt indebted to Chapman for her kindness and counsel throughout times of adversity and drew strength in their friendship.

"Now it is given to us to rejoice together in the fruition of our hopes and the fulfillment of our desires. It is not a triumph of persons but principles, and we rejoice and give thanks, not as partisans or victors, but for our dear country's sake and the cause of freedom and humanity throughout the world," he told her.[345]

In the years after the Civil War, Chapman stepped back from much of her public advocacy, though she continued with her writing and supported efforts to deliver aid to freed Blacks and advocate for women's rights. In addition to doling out practical advice to her children, her letters adopted a more philosophical tone—she was, after all, not just an abolitionist firebrand but also now a doting grandmother. "A born children's friend and entertainer," one grandson later described her.[346]

Her youngest daughter's marriage, her brother's illness, the birth of new grandchildren all now consumed much of her time. "I have been of necessity devoted to family causes and duties," she explained to a British abolitionist.[347]

Chapman helped her friend Harriet Martineau write her multi-volume autobiography, which was published posthumously in 1877, and recounted in detail the events surrounding the Gentlemen's Mob of 1835. The following year, Garrison and local abolitionists hosted a hastily planned event marking the forty-third anniversary of the event, which also coincided with the death of George Thompson.[348] Chapman was not able to attend, but she remained fiercely protective of the abolitionists' legacy and took great umbrage at what she felt were revisionist attempts by latecomers to the movement to claim their mantle.

In particular, she objected to efforts by Theodore Lyman III to defend his late father's role in the 1835 mob. His effort generated a heated exchange of letters, charges and countercharges between abolitionists and defenders of the former mayor. Lyman's son was "sewing the libraries of historical societies with cooked stories of things that took place while he was yet in his cradle," Chapman complained.[349] Garrison agreed. The 1835 anti-abolitionist mob had been described by many names over the years—the Boston Mob, the Ruffle Shirt Mob, the Garrison Mob, the Broadcloth Mob, the Gentlemen's Mob—but he felt it should be known more properly as the Lyman Mob. "This is simply 'calling things by their right names' and 'putting the boot on the right leg,'" Garrison wrote.[350]

Lyman was not the only one in Chapman's crosshairs. She also singled out her former minister, Reverend Channing, a vocal slavery opponent who, she felt, supported the abolitionists only in words—and not deeds—until it was politically convenient and socially acceptable to do so. She blamed him for condoning the mob and believed many of the leading "gentlemen" in the streets back in 1835 hailed from his church pews. It irked her that Reverend Channing was now held out as an antislavery champion. While it may be true that he had spoken out against the Lovejoy murder and later been helpful to the cause in other ways, he had been "timid and vacillating" when it really mattered, in her eyes.

"Facts are not always truths—for when they form but a part of truth they carry the power of a lie," she wrote, in a pointed critique of her former minister.[351]

For Chapman, the events of October 21, 1835, left an indelible mark and served as a crucible that still shaped her uncompromising view of the entire antislavery movement. She also felt a heightened sense of duty to defend the abolitionist legacy after the death of Thompson in 1878 and then Garrison in May of 1879.

Writing to another former abolitionist in 1881, Chapman still vividly recalled even the smallest details of the Gentlemen's Mob nearly half a century later. She remained incensed by attempts to reframe the mayor's confrontation with her in the hall at the women's antislavery meeting. "We saw [Mayor Lyman], pale with terror, ordering us out of our own hall at the command of a mob," she recalled with disgust.

While her sharp mind and strong views showed few signs of abating, Chapman's life had slowed in most other respects as the fiftieth anniversary approached in 1885. She lived quietly in Weymouth with her surviving sisters and family and kept up correspondence with her old abolitionist friends but otherwise lived mostly as a recluse.

By the summer of 1885, Chapman began to experience "gastric difficulty" and lost her appetite. She felt weak and remained confined to bed while her sisters and her doctor tended to her. They offered hot brandy to help soothe her ailments and keep her comfortable. Despite her frail condition, Chapman rarely complained and was still able to write several letters.

By the second Sunday of July, she was able to sit up in the morning and take a small bowl of milk porridge. Her sisters were pleased that she was able to hold the bowl herself and drink it normally. Later that morning, as her sisters helped to change her clothing, Chapman suddenly turned faint. Her sisters offered her water and rubbed her with cologne and brandy, while calling for the doctor.

Chapman lifted a small glass bottle and asked her sister to wipe down her face, but her hands trembled, and she had difficulty holding it. Her sister took the glass bottle and began to wipe her face—but "then came the change and I saw it was not faintness but death," Deborah Weston recalled. "The doctor came in at that moment and said it was over."[352]

Maria Weston Chapman died on Sunday, July 12, 1885, just shy of her seventy-ninth birthday. Officially, the cause of death was listed as heart disease.

The following spring, a celebration of Chapman's life was hosted by "old-time" abolitionists at a Unitarian church in Melrose. There were only a handful of survivors of the Gentlemen's Mob remaining, and they were joined by a contingent of the younger generation of antislavery activists, including William Lloyd Garrison Jr., who gave a lecture in Chapman's memory.

A group of abolitionists gathered at the home of Lucy Stone in the summer of 1886. *Left to right*: Samuel May, William Lloyd Garrison Jr., Elizabeth Chase, Francis Garrison, Sarah Southwick, Alla Foster, Harriet Sewall, Lucy Stone, Samuel Sewall, George Garrison, Zilpha Spooner, Wendell Garrison, Henry Blackwell and Theodore Weld. Some, like Southwick and Sewall, experienced the Gentlemen's Mob firsthand. *Smith College Special Collections.*

Among those in attendance was Sarah Southwick, who as a young teenager was trapped in the crowd outside the antislavery office, while her mother remained inside with Chapman, Susan Paul and the other women of the Boston Anti-Slavery Society. Another guest was the eighty-plus-year-old Samuel Sewall, who had been in the crowd and later visited Garrison at the jail after his escape from the mob. Samuel May, another octogenarian who was one of Garrison's oldest friends, also spoke and declared that without Chapman's assistance, he believed Garrison would have fallen in his life's work.[353]

After the speeches, a series of letters was read in Chapman's honor, many from guests who were unable to attend in person. They praised her leadership, drive and dedication and reminisced about the fateful Gentlemen's Mob and the early days of the abolition movement, agreeing that "of this band she was the recognized queen."

Three decades after his death, a bronze sculpture of Wendell Phillips was cast and unveiled in the Boston Public Garden, a short distance from where the rampaging anti-abolition mob once gathered. Phillips is depicted standing with a broken chain in his left hand and his right fist tightly clenched. The day after the dedication ceremony, a Boston writer artfully summed up the event—and Phillips's career: "Today there is a monument in Boston to Wendell Phillips. It is not a statue in the Public Garden. It is a memory and a hope in the hearts of living women and men."[354]

Chapman bust by Edmonia Lewis, 1865. *Author photo, Tufts Library Weymouth.*

There is no such statute of Maria Chapman featured in the Boston Public Garden, but in her hometown of Weymouth, Massachusetts, a life-size bust greets visitors in the town library, located near the site of her former home. Her memory also lives on in the generations of young students who pass through the Maria Weston Chapman Middle School, dedicated in 2004. A brand-new Chapman school will soon open, in time for a future graduating class to mark two hundred years since Maria Chapman's courageous stand for freedom against the Boston Gentlemen's Mob.

A NOTE ON SOURCES

They say that newspapers are the first rough draft of history, and that has certainly proven true here. Since much of my research took place during a pandemic, online access was a godsend. I relied extensively on the archives of the *Liberator* and many other newspapers, some of which are subscription based. These include genealogybank.com, Google news archive, newspapers.com, newspaperarchive.com, Boston Public Library newspapers (and their many other periodical collections) and Accessible Archives. I also consulted Nilesregister.com, the Massachusetts State Library, Library of Congress, Old Colony Library Network and the Boston Athenaeum.

For the perspective of Maria Weston Chapman, I relied primarily on the Weston sisters' diaries and letters, as well as the annual reports of the Boston Female Anti-Slavery Society. The diaries of Deborah Weston and Caroline Weston offer rich details of the events in the fall of 1835, including the days leading up and immediately after the abolition riot. For these diaries, and an extensive collection of correspondence, I relied on the BPL, Digital Commonwealth, and the Massachusetts Historical Society. Other letters were accessed through Smith College Special Collections and Harvard's Houghton Library. Additional details came from accounts published later, including Harriet Martineau's biography.

The *Papers of the Garrison Mob* by Theodore Lyman's son also provided an invaluable source, whether one considers it an attempt at revisionist history (as Chapman and the abolitionists did) or just setting the record straight.

This volume includes a personal narrative from the mayor not previously published. We don't know for sure when Mayor Lyman wrote this account, but his son reports that it was found among his papers and written in his own handwriting. The *Papers* also include some additional eyewitness recollections from key participants, though most were written long after the actual event.

The lengthy career of Wendell Phillips is well chronicled, but pinpointing his actions in the fall of 1835 is more challenging. What little we know of his experiences as a spectator comes mostly from his later speeches, including his "Boston Mob" speech given in 1855. He also wrote a newspaper account of his recollections that day, published in 1870. I relied on his letters and other abolitionist correspondence to augment this, most from the Boston Public Library and Harvard's Houghton Library.

Garrison's children compiled a comprehensive biography of their father in 1885, published in multiple volumes. This is not an original source per se, but it includes excerpts from some letters not accessible or preserved elsewhere. I relied primarily on volume two, which covers the 1835–40 period.

Earlier, I said the fun part of this project was stitching together sources to bring a narrative alive. I should add that it can also be frustrating when the historical record is lacking. That is certainly the case with Susan Paul, a remarkable woman who is deserving of a fuller treatment. Her work with children's choirs is chronicled in academic journals, several of which I included in the bibliography, and her *Memoir of James Jackson*, as published by Lois Brown, is also an excellent resource. A handful of her letters have survived, and some are accessible from the Boston Public Library's helpful Digital Commonwealth website. Further details came from the archives of the *Liberator* and correspondence of other abolitionists.

All quoted conversations, unless otherwise noted, are based on these primary sources. In limited cases where witnesses had conflicting recollections, I have either presented each side or made an editorial judgment as to which account was more credible based on the available evidence. Whenever possible, I have also corroborated key points of witness testimony with other accounts and known facts. Conversations are recalled verbatim, though in a few cases, I have cleaned up the punctuation for the sake of clarity or readability.

An indispensable almanac of city residents containing addresses, occupations, street listings, businesses and census data is Stimpson's Boston Directory. I relied primarily on the 1834, 1835 and 1836 editions, accessible via hathitrust.org and the Boston Athenaeum. For details on locations, streets and other period details, I also relied on Bowen's Boston. Weather-related details are based on contemporary newspaper accounts. For details on Garrison's arraignment, I relied on the original police court docket entries for October 1835, provided courtesy of the Boston City Archives.

Early on, I found several previously published works particularly helpful to my research and would like to thank authors Lee Chambers, Henry Mayer and Debra Hansen and editor Walter Merrill. Patrick Browne's history blog (historicaldigression.com) has an excellent entry on "The Garrison Mob of 1835, Boston," and the late Horace Seldon's website, "The Liberator Files" (www.theliberatorfiles.com), is another great resource. Thank you to the Seldon family for keeping his legacy going.

A lengthy bibliography is listed at the end of this book. The endnotes offer an abridged version of sources used in this narrative, primarily to give credit to other authors, secondary sources and compiled collections of primary sources. Due to space restrictions, I have not included reference notes for every source. More information is available at www.garrisonmob.com.

NOTES

Chapter 1

1. Southwick, *Reminiscences*, 29.
2. Garrison letter to BFASS, April 9, 1834; Mary Grew letter to Garrison, April 11, 1834, Massachusetts Historical Society (MHS).
3. Ibid.
4. *Liberator*, April 16, 1831, 63.
5. Ibid., April 20, 1835, 3; Brown, ed. *Memoirs of James Jackson*, 15; Horton and Horton, *Black Bostonians*, 32.
6. *Liberator*, March 29, 1834, 3.
7. Susan Paul letter to Garrison, April 1, 1834, Boston Public Library (BPL).

Chapter 2

8. Lyman, *Papers*, 15.
9. Ibid.
10. "Proceedings of the Dedication of the Fountain on Eaton Square," 38.
11. The newspaper's shelf life was brief, though successful, and it ceased publication shortly after Jackson was elected president in December 1828. Lyman's tenure as a newspaper publisher might have been more noteworthy for an article published in October 1828 critical of U.S. senator Daniel Webster. The article implied that Webster had formerly supported dissolving the Union. Webster took offense at the perceived betrayal and sought criminal charges against Lyman. The grand jury obliged, and Lyman was indicted for two counts of criminal libel a few weeks later. The case, which drew national attention, went to trial the following month, and Lyman escaped prosecution thanks to a hung jury. See Benton, *Notable Libel Case*.

12. *Salem Gazette*, December 12, 1834, 2; *Columbian Register*, November 20, 1834, 3; *Daily Atlas*, November 20, 1834, 2.

13. Massachusetts General Court, "Free Negroes and Mulattoes," True and Green Printers, January 16, 1822.

14. There is no record of the vote in surviving accounts of council minutes, a curious omission in itself, but the decision was noted in contemporary press accounts. Mayor Lyman, as ex-officio chairman of the board of aldermen, would have necessarily played a role in the decision.

15. *New Bedford Gazette*, June 1, 1835, 1.

16. *Liberator*, June 6, 1835, 1; August 15, 1835, 1.

17. Ibid., June 13, 1835, 1, quoting *Boston Commercial Gazette*.

18. *Norfolk Advertiser* (Dedham, MA), July 7, 1835, 3; *Baltimore Gazette*, July 27, 1835, 2; *Independent Chronicle* (Boston), August 8, 1835, 2; *Commercial Advertiser* (NY), August 23, 1835, 2.

19. More recent commentators have dubbed it the nation's "first direct mail campaign." See Smithsonian National Postal Museum, postalmuseum.si.edu/node/1912.

20. *Southern Patriot* (Charleston, SC), "Incendiary Publications," July 30, 1835, 2.

21. *Weekly Raleigh Register* (North Carolina), August 4, 1835, 2, quoting *Nashville Banner*. For Mississippi insurrection scare, see also Morris, "Event in Community Organization," 93–111.

22. *Boston Investigator*, August 7, 1835, 2, quoting *Boston Morning Post*.

23. Notice and list of petitioners published in *Boston Daily Advertiser*, August 18, 1835, 2; for breakdown of petitioners by occupation and income level, see Hammett, "Two Mobs of Jacksonian Boston."

24. *Columbian Centinel*, "Meteorological Journal for August, 1835," September 5, 1835, 4.

25. *Washington Globe*, August 27, 1835, 2, quoting *Boston Courier*.

26. *Liberator*, September 29, 1835, 3, quoting *New England Spectator*.

27. *National Intelligencer* (Washington, D.C.), "Speech of Richard Fletcher, Esq.," August 29, 1835, 2.

28. Ibid.

29. *Charleston Courier*, "Faneuil Hall Meeting," September 3, 1835, 2.

Chapter 3

30. Deborah Weston Diaries, July 22, 1835, BPL.

31. For more on elder Chapman's decision to sacrifice his southern mercantile business in protest of slavery, see *Liberator*, "Henry Chapman, Esq.," December 4, 1846, 2; Wilson, *Aristocracy of Boston*, 11.

32. Southwick, *Reminiscences*, 85.

33. Edmund Quincy. See Taylor, *Women of the Anti-Slavery Movement*, 12 (quoted in).

34. For more on this, see Hyde, "West Street."

35. In a twist of fate, Susan Paul's uncle, Reverend Nathaniel Paul, deserves some credit for bringing the two men together. Reverend Paul traveled to Liverpool

in 1832 for an extended visit and befriended Thompson. He also shared copies of the *Liberator* with Thompson prior to Garrison's arrival in London in May 1833. Another aside of note: Garrison used Reverend Paul's marriage to a white woman in London as further evidence of Britain's more progressive and tolerant views on race. "What an uproar such an occurrence would create in this country. Even in Massachusetts, the marriage would by law be null and void, and the clergymen performing it would be fined £50!" he wrote. See *First Annual Report of the Board of Managers of the New England Anti-Slavery Society*, Garrison & Knapp, 1833, 34; and Nathaniel Paul letter to Garrison, August 31, 1833, BPL. (Note the letter is dated August 31, 1833, but this would seem impossible. Garrison was already in the UK since May of that year, and the letter was addressed to William Lloyd Garrison, of Boston, America. The letter dateline is partially obscured and more likely was written August 31, 1832.)

36. Caroline Weston diary, September 19, 1835, BPL.
37. Ibid., September 16, 1835.
38. Deborah Weston diary, July 29, 1835, BPL.
39. Several men were later charged with breaking windows at the church. Thompson returned in mid-October for another lecture, which went off without any reported incident. Deborah Weston diary, September 28, 1835, BPL; *Liberator*, November 10, 1835, 3; *Norfolk Advertiser*, November 17, 1835, 2; *Collection of Historical Papers on Abington*, Abington Women's Club, 1930, Dyer Memorial Library.
40. *Commercial Advertiser* (NY), September 28, 1835, 2; *Spectator* (NY), October 1, 1835, 1; *Jeffersonian* (ME), October 19, 1835; *Baltimore Gazette and Daily Advertiser*, October 7, 1835, 2; *Eastern Argus* (ME), October 21, 1835, 2; *New Bedford Gazette*, October 5, 1835, 2; *Alexandria Gazette*, October 19, 1835, 2; *Albany Argus*, October 20, 1835, 3. See denial in *New Hampshire Statesmen*, October 24, 1835, 1, quoting *Commercial Advertiser*.
41. *Liberator*, September 19, 1835, 2; August 29, 1835, 3.
42. Deborah Weston diary, September 20, 1835, BPL.
43. Caroline Weston diary, October 2, 1835, BPL.
44. Chapman is occasionally cited as one of the twelve women who founded the Boston Female Anti-Slavery Society in October 1833, but it is more likely she became active with the group later. The society's original president was Charlotte Phelps, whose husband, Reverend Amos Phelps, had helped guide the new group, but she moved away, and Susan Grew took over as president in early 1834. Martha Ball was the first recording secretary, and other early board members included Catherine Sullivan, Heidi White and Mary Grew. The women formally adopted a constitution at their April 1834 meeting, which included ten board positions, one of which was awarded to Susan Paul. In a letter Mary Grew wrote to Charlotte Phelps on April 12, 1834, she offered an update on the society's progress and included a list of the current BFASS members, including three life members and forty-two annual subscribers, but Chapman was not listed among them. According to Sarah Southwick, Chapman did not join BFASS until July 1835 (Southwick, *Reminiscences*, 9). This comports with Deborah Weston's diary

entry of July 22, 1835. There is also additional circumstantial evidence based on some of Chapman's and BFASS's letters. (See Chapman to Anne Warren Weston, Tuesday morning [December 1834], BPL; Chapman to Elizabeth Pease Nichol, January 28, 1854, Smith College; and Boston Female Anti-Slavery Society Letterbook, 1834–38, MHS.) Chapman and her sister Anne may have taken on the role of corresponding secretary at this July 1835 meeting following the departure of Mary Grew, who moved to Philadelphia. Chapman was initially in charge of "foreign" correspondence, while her sister handled the "domestic" correspondence. See also *Liberator*, November 1, 1835, 4.

45. Beginning around October 1835, Julien Hall became known as Congress Hall. For most of the fall, it was referred to as "Congress Hall (formerly Julien Hall)" in most newspapers, though some accounts continued to refer to Julien Hall for longer. Bowen's *Picture of Boston* 1838 refers to it as Congress Hall. The BFASS meeting notice and most contemporary accounts referred to Congress Hall, which is we why have used that label here.

46. Caroline Weston diary, October 11, 1835, BPL.

47. *Columbia Centinel*, October 14, 1835, 2.

48. *Boston Courier*, October 14, 1835, 2, quoting *Boston Commercial Gazette*.

49. *Richmond Enquirer* (VA), October 20, 1835, 4.

50. *Right and Wrong*, 1835, 11.

51. *Boston Courier*, October 14, 1835, 2.

52. Deborah Weston diary, October 13, 1835, BPL.

53. *Liberator*, October 17, 1835, 2. A notice had run in the October 10, 1835 issue of the *Liberator* listing New Jerusalem Church as the location for the Female Anti-Slavery Society meeting. See also *Right and Wrong*, 1835, 9.

54. Deborah Weston diary, October 13, 1835, BPL.

55. *Weekly Messenger*, October 15, 1835, 3.

56. Deborah Weston diary, October 14, 1835, BPL.

57. *Liberator*, October 17, 1835, 2.

58. *Right and Wrong*, 1835, 26; *Washington Globe* (D.C.), October 24, 1835, quoting *Boston Atlas*.

59. In Deborah Weston's diary that day she wrote: "The piece by a member of the Boston Female A.S. appeared in the Courier this morning." It's unclear if she was unaware that Maria played a role in writing the article, purposefully omitted it or just that Maria did not in fact have a hand in writing it.

60. Deborah Weston diary, October 17, 1835, BPL.

61. Chapman letter to unknown, October 17, 1835, BPL.

62. The conversation was retold by Scottish abolitionist Eliza Wigham. Her narrative presented the woman's comments in quotation marks, though she was clearly not present at the time and must have relied on Maria Chapman to recount. See Wigham, *Anti-Slavery Cause in America.*

63. *Salem Gazette*, October 20, 1835, 1; *Newburyport Herald*, October 20, 1835, 2; *Boston Courier*, October 18, 1835, 3; *Boston Traveller*, October 20, 1835, 2; *Saturday Morning Transcript*, October 17, 1835, 3.

64. Deborah Weston diary, October 19, 1835, BPL.

65. *Boston Journal*, "The 'Lyman' Mob' Lecture by Wendell Phillips," November 17, 1870, 4.

66. Letter from Deborah Weston to Aunt Mary, October 22, 1835, BPL (typed transcript).

67. Garrison and Garrison, *William Lloyd Garrison*, Vol. 2, 10–11.

68. *Boston Sunday Budget*, "The Garrison Mob," March 18, 1883.

69. Yerrinton, *Proceedings*, 24.

70. Garrison and Garrison, *William Lloyd Garrison*, Vol. 2, 8, quoting letter to George Benson.

Chapter 4

71. Austin, *Life and Times*, 44.

72. Martyn, *Wendell Phillips*, 43, quoting Edgar Buckingham.

73. Congdon, *Reminiscences of a Journalist*, 59.

74. *Harvard Illustrated Magazine*, January 1900, 183.

75. Ibid.

76. Austin, *Life and Times*, 39.

77. *Boston Globe*, "To the Memory of Wendell Phillips," Remarks of Benjamin F. Butler, February 4, 1884, 1. See also Stewart, *Wendell Phillips*, 42.

78. Garrison and Garrison, *William Lloyd Garrison*, Vol. 2, 8, quoting *Boston Sunday Budget*, March 18, 1883.

79. Speech given on the twentieth anniversary of mob attack. Phillips, *Speeches, Lectures and Letters*, 213.

80. Ibid.

81. Oliver, et al., *Proceedings*, 340, quoting Representative Ellis Ames.

82. Ibid., 342.

83. *Boston Sunday Budget*, "The Garrison Mob," March 18, 1883.

Chapter 5

84. For more on Burleigh see Brown, "Antislavery Agent."

85. Garrison, *Helen Eliza Garrison*, 25.

86. *Right and Wrong*, 1835, 30.

87. Southwick, *Reminiscences*, 11.

88. Caroline Weston letter to Wendell Phillips, Weymouth, October 27, [1870], Blagden Collection, Harvard University.

89. *Liberator*, October 24, 1835, 3.

90. Garrison and Garrison, *William Lloyd Garrison*, Vol. 2, 8, quoting *Boston Sunday Budget*, March 18, 1883, 12.

91. *Right and Wrong*, 1835, 30.

92. Garrison and Garrison, *William Lloyd Garrison*, Vol. 2, 13.

93. Deborah Weston letter to Aunt Mary, October 22, 1835, BPL (typed transcript).
94. *Right and Wrong*, 1835, 31.

Chapter 6

95. Ibid., 34.
96. Maria Chapman letter to Reverend Samuel May, June 3, 1881, BPL.
97. Some commentators have deemed these often-quoted words apocryphal, but it seems likely that Chapman did utter something substantially similar. Chapman herself reports the exchange in the 1835 annual report, which she emphasizes was a verbatim reporting: "We record no 'imaginary conversation.' The following is, word for word, what passed between him, the President and other ladies." Mayor Lyman's own account, while not offering as much detail, does add credence to her remarks: "One said in substance, that if it was necessary to die in that cause, they might as well die there and then." See *Right and Wrong*, 1835, and *Papers*.
98. It was Francis Jackson. See Yerrinton, *Proceedings*, 4.
99. *Columbian Centinel*, October 24, 1835, 1.

Chapter 7

100. Proceedings of the Massachusetts Historical Society, Vol. 18, February Meeting, 1881, 340, quoting Representative Ellis Ames, 341.
101. Ibid., 251.
102. *Liberator*, October 24, 1835.
103. Recounted by Charles Burleigh. *Liberator*, October 24, 1835.
104. *Boston Morning Post*, October 23, 1835, 2.
105. *Zion's Herald*, October 27, 1835, 170; *Salem Gazette*, October 23, 1835, 2.
106. Tiffany, *Sewall*, 46, quoting letter from Sewall to Louisa M. Winslow, October 22, 1835.
107. The sign has been identified in various sources as the Female Abolition Society Room, Anti-Slavery Office(s) and the Anti-Slavery Rooms. Maria Chapman in her report makes clear it was Rooms. See *Right and Wrong*, 56.
108. Lyman, *Papers*, 41.
109. Ibid., 19.
110. *Liberator*, October 31, 1835, 3.
111. *Boston Sunday Budget*, "The Garrison Mob," March 18, 1883.
112. Tiffany, *Sewall*, 47.
113. *Woman's Journal*, October 26, 1878, 340.
114. *Liberator*, "Triumph of Mobocracy in Boston," November 7, 1835, 2.

Chapter 8

115. *Liberator*, November 24, 1835.

116. The request would later be the subject of some controversy. According to Lyman's account, Garrison had agreed to climb the attic stairs to conceal himself there. But Garrison supporters later pointed out that there were no stairs to the attic—a picayune detail but emblematic of the broader disagreement between the Garrison and Lyman camp narratives. See *Boston Daily Advertiser*, "The Boston Mob of 1885," November 17, 1870; Lyman, *Papers*, 19.

117. *Liberator*, "Triumph of Mobocracy in Boston," November 17, 1835, 2.

118. Ibid., November 7, 1835, 2.

119. For details on Luke Brown and the events at his carpentry shop, see *Boston Journal*, "How Garrison Was Saved," as published in *Daily Evening Bulletin* (San Francisco), September 24, 1887, 3; *Boston Herald*, "The Garrison Mob," as published in *Cleveland Leader and Herald*, October 6, 1890. For a helpful compendium of the Luke Brown accounts, see North Bridgeton Historical Society, "Luke Brown's Abolition Hotbed," www.northbridgtonhistorical.org/luke-brown.

120. *Boston Journal*, "How Garrison Was Saved."

121. The barber was Francis Ashton, originally Francisco Astorini. See *Saturday Morning Transcript*, December 27, 1834, 2; *Boston Globe*, October 22, 1890, 1.

122. Fuller later became an active abolitionist and regretted his role in the mob. He recounted his story to a newspaper reporter while visiting a bronze statue to the late Garrison on the fifty-fifth anniversary of the event. "I came to tell this story to Garrison, but he will not hear." See *Boston Globe*, October 22, 1890, 1.

123. Garrison later identified a Joseph K. Hayes as the man who closed the doors of the shop and "gallantly endeavored to keep the mob back." It is likely that Hayes is the same person identified by other witnesses as an apprentice holding the axe.

124. *Boston Sunday Budget*, March 18, 1883.

125. Various crowd reactions reported in *Boston Evening Transcript*, March 12, 1884, 6; *Boston Commonwealth*, October 23, 1880.

126. *Niles Register*, November 21, 1835, 194, quoting *Boston Evening Transcript*.

127. Garrison and Garrison, *William Lloyd Garrison*, Vol. 2, 21, quoting manuscript found among Garrison's papers.

128. *Boston Commonwealth*, October 23, 1880.

129. Garrison and Garrison, *William Lloyd Garrison*, Vol. 2, 21.

Chapter 9

130. *Liberator*, October 24, 1835.

131. Thirty Truckmen letter to Garrison and Isaac Knapp, [1835?], BPL.

132. Tiffany, *Sewall*, 49.

133. Letter from Deborah Weston to Mary Weston, Thursday noon, [October 22, 1835], BPL. Samuel Sewall also mentioned Cooley in his firsthand account. See Tiffany, *Sewall*, 49.

134. Cooley fell on hard times and wrote a series of letters to Garrison, Wendell Phillips and other abolitionists asking for money. See Epilogue.

135. *Boston Investigator*, June 16, 1886, 4.

136. The *Boston Transcript* cited an unidentified witness who refuted abolitionist claims and said there was actually no crowd pressing against Garrison. He appeared anything but calm and was "deadly pale whilst a ghastly smile was diffused over his pallid features." See *Boston Spectator*, November 11, 1835, 2, quoting *Boston Transcript*.

137. Recounted by Wendell Phillips in his lecture on the "Lyman Mob." See *Boston Journal*, October 17, 1870, 4.

138. Lyman, *Papers*, 44.

139. *Liberator*, November 17, 1835, 2.

140. Lyman, *Papers*, 42.

141. Ibid., 70, quoting "New York Lecture, Nov. 16."

142. Ibid., 54.

143. Oliver et al., *Proceedings*, Vol. 18, 341.

144. Lyman, *Papers*, 22.

Chapter 10

145. *Liberator*, December 20, 1834, 3; *Boston Daily Advertiser*, December 16, 1834, 2.

146. Garrison to his wife, December 30, 1835, quoted in Merrill, *Letters*, 592.

147. They ultimately scheduled the fair for December 23, 1835, at the home of Maria Chapman's father-in-law, Henry Chapman, on Chauncy Place. The second annual event was hosted over a period of two days but was not publicly advertised, and the sales were somewhat of a disappointment. The proceeds were recorded as either $600, according to the *Liberator*, or $343, per a later accounting of Caroline Weston.

148. Garrison regularly hired young Black men to apprentice at his newspaper, an uncommon practice at the time. Another young *Liberator* apprentice (who may also have been a student of Susan Paul's) and later went on to prominence was William C. Nell.

149. The *Liberator* published a brief but glowing death notice of Ann Paul Smith accompanied by Bible verse, noting that she died after "a short and distressing illness, which she bore with Christian meekness and fortitude....In the death of Mrs. Smith, the colored population have met with a loss that will be long and severely felt." Coincidentally, the notice was published in the same issue as the first excerpts of Susan Paul's James Jackson memoir. See *Liberator*, June 17, 1835, 3–4.

150. One of the early notices was in *Boston Recorder*, May 29, 1835, 4.

151. Brown, *Memoirs of James Jackson*.

152. Its broader significance would not be recognized until much later. Some historians credit Paul as the first African American woman to publish a biography. Ibid.

153. *Essex North Register and Family Monitor*, August 20, 1835, 2.

154. The area west of the Commons, once described as "patches of swamp grass and weeds, with an occasional puddle of water," later became the Boston Public

Gardens. Preliminary plans were approved by the city council in October 1837. See Ayer, *Early Days on Boston Common*; *Columbian Centinel*, October 28, 1837, 2; *Boston Courier*, November 23, 1837, 2; Barber, *Boston Common*.

155. Recollection of Benjamin C. Bacon. See Johnson and Whittier, *William Lloyd Garrison*, 88.

Chapter 11

156. Caroline Weston letter to Wendell Phillips, Weymouth, October 27, [1870], Blagden Collection, Harvard University.

157. Garrison later offered his own forceful denial, telling Wendell Phillips in a letter that Lyman's claim about him seeking to avoid any expense was "utterly false" and "almost too ridiculous to deny." See Garrison letter to Wendell Phillips, November 1870, Blagden Collection, Houghton Library.

158. *Boston Commonwealth*, October 23, 1880.

159. Deborah Weston letter to Mary Weston, October 22, 1835, BPL.

160. Ibid.

161. Oliver et al., *Proceedings*, Vol. 18.

162. Tiffany, *Sewall*, 51.

163. Buffum recounted this story during an event marking the fiftieth anniversary of the mob attack. He also shared an anecdote about his experiences traveling with abolitionist leader Frederick Douglass when the pair were both denied passage on a train bound from Lynn to Newburyport. Buffum stuck up for his friend Douglass and was called a racial epithet. The pejorative nickname stuck on Buffum for a period, which he noted with irony since he was later elected mayor of the city and was now addressed as "Honorable James." See *Boston Daily Advertiser*, October 22, 1885, 8.

164. *Boston Globe*, October 22, 1890, 1.

165. *Boston Daily Advertiser*, October 22, 1890, 8.

166. The boy was Lowell Mason Jr., son of Lowell Mason, the acclaimed musician and founder of the Boston Academy of Music. Mason Jr. later followed in his father's footsteps as a successful religious music publisher. Anecdote cited in Garrison and Garrison, *William Lloyd Garrison*, Vol. 2, 27. Original source is unknown.

167. *Liberator*, December 12, 1835, 1.

168. Ibid.

Chapter 12

169. Maria Chapman recalled the comment from Stephen Rhoades, who owned a hat store on Court Street. See Chapman letter to Francis Jackson Garrison, August 9, 1881, BPL.

170. *Woman's Journal*, October 27, 1878, 340.

171. Lyman, *Papers*, 40.

172. Pierce, *Memoir*, 147.

173. Oliver et al., *Proceedings*, Vol. 18, 342–43.

174. Charles Sumner to Cornelius Felton, April 9, 1850, Sumner Papers, Harvard, as quoted in Taylor, *Young Charles Sumner*, 72.

175. Letter to Dr. Francis Lieber, January 9, 1836, as quoted in Pierce, *Memoir*, 153.

176. Bowditch reported that he subscribed to the *Liberator* the next day. See *Boston Daily Advertiser*, October 17, 1881, 4.

177. Mayer, *All on Fire*, 382, quoting Edmund Quincy Diary, October 21, 1835.

178. Adams Papers, Diary of Charles Francis Adams, vol. 6, Massachusetts Historical Society, www.masshist.org/publications/adams-papers/index.php/view/ADMS-13-06-02-0002-0010-0023

179. *Right and Wrong*, 1835, 39.

Chapter 13

180. Tiffany, *Sewall*, 48.

181. Lyman, *Papers*, 24.

182. *Boston Recorder*, January 2, 1835, 4; Drake, *Old Landmarks*, 78–79; *Lighthouse* (Salem, MA), June 1, 1835.

183. *Salem Gazette*, October 16, 1835, 3; *Trumpet and Universalist Magazine*, June 20, 1835, 2.

184. Quoted comments were shared in a letter from Garrison to Wendell Phillips written much later but substantively similar to his contemporary comments in the *Liberator*. See Garrison letter to Wendell Phillips, November 1870, Blagden Collection, Harvard University.

185. Ibid.

186. Grimké, *William Lloyd Garrison*, 231.

187. Emerson's journal entry of October 21, 1835, reports his meeting with Alcott, a fellow transcendentalist, whom he described as "a wise man, simple, superior to display, and drops the best things as quietly as the least." The Alcotts' daughter, Louisa May, just two years old at the time, would later go on to write a series of books, including *Little Women*. See Emerson, *Journals*, 559; *Woman's Journal*, October 27, 1878, 340.

188. Tiffany, *Sewall*, 43.

189. Lyman, *Papers*, 65–68.

190. Deborah Weston letter to Aunt Mary, October 22, 1835, BPL.

191. This conversation is recounted by Harriet Martineau in an article first published in 1838 in the UK. The visitors were not identified except as "several gentlemen," some of whom Chapman knew from Dr. Channing's church. We can't say with any certainty that this group was the Homer, Williams and Davenport group, though the timing and substance of the conversation comports to what was described in the Weston sisters' correspondence. Dr. Channing was the well-known minister of the Unitarian church on Federal

Street where the Chapmans were members, along with a number of the city's "gentlemen of property and standing." His views were generally progressive, and he vigorously opposed slavery, but he did not originally agree with the abolitionists' immediate emancipation position and was occasionally critical of their efforts, which caused conflict and eventually a permanent rift with Chapman. See Martineau, *Martyr Age*. Relevant portions also published in *Boston Courier*, February 4, 1839.

192. Deborah Weston diary, October 21, 1835, BPL.

Chapter 14

193. Nell, *Colored Patriots*.

194. Pittsburgh Resolutions, September 1, 1831, as published in James Cropper, *A Letter to Thomas Clarkson*, London, 1832.

195. The future Mrs. George Vashon was Susan Paul Smith, the young niece of Susan Paul, who was now helping to raise her after her mother's untimely death several months earlier. Vashon and Smith ultimately married two decades later after meeting as adults in Pittsburgh, but their common abolitionist ties and Garrison friendship no doubt played a matchmaking role.

196. Davis, *History of the Judiciary of Massachusetts*, 218.

197. Police Court Docket, City of Boston Archives, October 1835.

198. Ibid.

199. *Liberator*, December 12, 1835, 1.

200. Police Court Docket, City of Boston Archives, October 1835.

201. Presumably, Garrison's wallet and letters were returned, since there was only one notice published. Many years later, Garrison received correspondence identifying the young man who had ended up with the papers as Spencer Vinal, who, coincidentally, was the son of his landlord at the time. The letter writer recounted to Garrison that Vinal "came home to his father's house in the evening to supper, wearing your coat, from a pocket of which he took a handful of papers and letters, saying, 'I have got the whole abolition correspondence, I guess.'" Vinal had joined in with the anti-abolitionist crowd and was no fan of Garrison, but he felt the mob had gone too far and may have joined with truckman Aaron Cooley in coming to his aid. See Thompson letter to Garrison, March 26, 1879, as quoted in Garrison and Garrison, *William Lloyd Garrison*, Vol. 2, 10–11, 24; letter from Garrison to Henry Benson, December 15, 1835, as published in Merrill, *Letters*, 575; and *Liberator*, November 21, 1835, 3.

202. Garrison, *Helen Eliza Garrison*, 39.

203. Letter from George Benson to William Lloyd Garrison, October 23, 1835, BPL.

204. Benson letter to George W. Benson, as quoted in Garrison and Garrison, *William Lloyd Garrison*, Vol. 2, 37.

Chapter 15

205. *Boston Daily Advertiser*, October 22, 1835, 2.
206. *Columbian Centinel*, October 21, 1835, 2.
207. *Boston Commercial Gazette*, October 10, 1835, as published in *United States Gazette* (Philadelphia), October 28, 1835, 4.
208. *Boston Atlas*, October 22, 1835, as quoted in *American Sentinel* (PA), October 26, 1835, 2.
209. *Boston Mercantile Journal*, as quoted in *Newburyport Herald*, October 27, 1835, 1.
210. *Boston Morning Post*, October 22, 1835, 2.
211. *Liberator*, November 7, 1835, 4, quoting *Boston Daily Advocate*.
212. *Boston Courier*, October 23, 1835, 2.
213. Isaac Knapp letter to Garrison, October 26, 1835, BPL.
214. Ibid.
215. The *Liberator* did not regularly publish circulation data, and there was certainly no independent auditing authority, so figures should be taken with a dose of skepticism. See *Liberator*, November 24, 1837, 2; February 8, 1834, 3; January 3, 1835, 3. An expanded accounting of the paper's circulation woes was included in a letter Garrison circulated to friends in April 1834 with the heading, "Shall the *Liberator* Die?" See Garrison and Garrison, *William Lloyd Garrison*, Vol. 1, 430–31.
216. *Liberator*, October 24, 1835, 3.
217. Ibid.
218. Anne Warren Weston letter to Mary Weston, October 27, 1835, BPL.
219. Ibid.
220. Ibid.
221. *Boston Courier*, October 27, 1835, 2; *Newburyport Morning Herald*, October 27, 1835, 2; *Boston Daily Advertiser*, October 28, 1835, 2; *Salem Gazette*, October 27, 1835, 3.
222. While in Salem, Thompson stayed at the home of a Mr. Spencer. After a few days, word of his location got out, and a mob organized to pursue him. Thompson was alerted and slipped away but left his family to the safety of the Spencers. That evening, a band of men collected in the streets and mobilized against the Spencers' home, demanding to know Thompson's location. They threw stones and made threats of violence. The attempted siege eventually petered out, but not before some tense moments for Mr. Spencer and his family. See Glasgow, *Three Years*, 18–19.
223. Hansen, *Strained Sisterhood*.
224. *Liberator*, November 7, 1835, 2.
225. Southwick, *Reminiscences*, 14–15.

Chapter 16

226. Lyman, *Papers*, 65.
227. Martineau, *Society in America*, 213.

228. Ibid., 129.

229. *Daily Memphis Avalanche* (TN), May 30, 1875, 2.

230. The Peterboro Presbyterian Church, where the reconvened meeting was held, is now home to the Abolition Hall of Fame and Museum.

231. May, *Some Recollections*, 153–55.

232. *Columbus Enquirer*, November 6, 1835, 4.

233. *Alexandria Gazette*, October 27, 1835, 3.

234. *North Carolina Standard*, November 5, 1835, 2.

235. President Andrew Jackson, Seventh Annual Message, December 8, 1835, as published by the American Presidency Project, www.presidency.ucsb.edu/documents/seventh-annual-message-2.

236. *Manchester Times*, November 28, 1835, 2.

237. *Belfast News-Letter* (Ireland), September 22, 1835, 1.

238. The causes of labor and antislavery advocates were not entirely aligned, but here their interests coalesced since the mob was composed primarily of the city's establishment class. A letter published by the *Reformer* from "A Working Man" aptly summed up this symbiosis: "I do not wish them to approve of the measures of Abolitionists. But let them rally for FREE DISCUSSION—the watchword of their hopes. How long will the restless spirit of the Aristocracy be content with an easy victory over the liberty of one defenseless man?" See *Liberator*, October 31, 1835, 2–3; Anne Weston letter to Mary Weston, October 30, 1835, BPL.

239. *Boston Courier*, August 13, 1834, 2.

Chapter 17

240. The first public primary school for Black students in Boston opened in 1820. It was housed in a room at the African Meeting House next to the existing grammar school for an annual rent of seventy-two dollars. There were forty-seven students to start, most aged four to seven years old. Two more (segregated) primary schools were opened soon after, but problems at Primary School No. 2 led city officials to dismiss the original teacher and replace her with Susan's mother, Catharine (sometimes Catherine) Waterhouse Paul. She moved the location from around the corner on Southac Street to an "airy and central" room in her own home on George Street. The move and her teaching abilities proved a successful match, and school enrollment grew quickly. "The school has a more orderly and cleanly appearance; and in the studies and manners of the children there is much improvement," the school committee noted. Susan Paul began her own teaching career in the family home along with her mother and continued thereafter. It's not entirely clear when the school moved out of the Paul family home, but it is likely that it relocated to the African Meeting House sometime after her father's death, before eventually landing at the adjacent new Smith School House. See Wightman, *Annals of the Boston Primary School Committee*, 94–96; and more generally Baumgartner, *In Pursuit of Knowledge*, 161–66; Levesque, "Before Integration," 113–25.

241. Yocum, "Smith School House," 64–68.

242. Ibid., 187, quoting report of Boston City Council, October 11, 1833, 401.

243. Minot, *Address.*

244. Garrison, *Abolitionist*, 126.

245. Published in *Liberator*, May 31, 1834, 3. For more background, see Brown, "Out of the Mouths of Babes," 52–79.

246. Garrison letter to Isaac Knapp, October 28, 1835, BPL.

247. See letters from Anne Weston to Mary Weston, October 27, 1835, and October 30, 1835, BPL; Charles Burleigh letter to Henry Benson, Boston, October 26, 1835, as quoted in Garrison and Garrison, *William Lloyd Garrison*, Vol. 2, 39.

248. Garrison and Garrison, *William Lloyd Garrison*, Vol. 2, 39.

249. Garrison adored cats but had an aversion to dogs, according to his son. See Garrison and Garrison, *William Lloyd Garrison*, Vol. 4, 312.

250. Tracking the Paul family's residences requires some sleuthing. Around 1823, the family moved from Belknap Street (Joy Street) to a three-floor gray brick home at 26 George Street (now 36 West Cedar Street), which now bears a plaque. Sometime after Reverend Paul's death in 1831, the family moved. City directory records for the years 1834 and 1836 show the family listed at 6 George Street, a few houses down from their prior home. It's not clear if this is simply a typo or an actual change in address. Given the family's changing financial fortunes and other circumstantial evidence, it's likely they did move soon after his death. Census records show that the Paul family lived in the same West End neighborhood (Ward 6) in 1830 and again in 1840 but do not pinpoint locations. For a time, the family lived on a street with mostly white neighbors because they could not find suitable housing in the more crowded Black section. That arrangement did not last when the neighbors apparently took offense, according to friend and author Lydia Maria Child. In 1837, Susan Paul and her family moved once again, this time to a home on Grove Street in the same area of Beacon Hill. See Meltzer, Holland and Krasno, *Lydia Maria Child*, 583; Grover and da Silva, "Historic Resource Study."

Chapter 18

251. Anne Warren Weston letter to Mary Weston, October 30, 1835, BPL.

252. Thompson letter to Henry Clarke Wright, November 25, 1835, BPL.

253. Garrison letter to Helen Garrison, November 9, 1835, as quoted in Garrison and Garrison, *William Lloyd Garrison*, Vol. 2, 49.

254. *Liberator*, December 5, 1835, 2.

255. Susan Paul letter to George Thompson, November 18, 1835, as published in Glasgow, *Three Years*, 22.

256. *Boston Daily Advertiser*, November 30, 1835, 2.

257. *Liberator*, November 21, 1835, 3.

258. Formal notice of the dissolution was published in the January 2, 1836 issue of the *Liberator*. Knapp had issues with alcohol, which have may have contributed to the breakup. He died in 1843. See *Liberator*, September 29, 1843, 2.

Chapman did not shy away from talk of disunion. Indeed, she was to join Garrison and other abolitionists for a national convention in Ohio in the fall of 1857 "to consider the practicality, probability and expediency of a separation of the Free and Slave States."[337] The formal convention was ultimately postponed, ostensibly due to the nation's pending financial crisis, but a number of delegates still met in October.

Even as the separation of the free and proslavery states became a reality, Chapman continued in her work. She followed events on the national stage carefully and, like Garrison, was deeply skeptical of the political newcomer Abraham Lincoln. "He will do nothing to offend the South," Garrison wrote

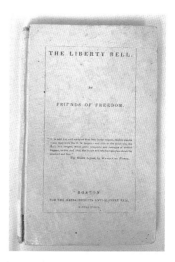

Liberty Bell cover. *Author photo, Tufts Library Weymouth.*

shortly before his election in 1860, and later called him "wishy-washy," a sentiment that Chapman would certainly have shared.[338] Both had previously eschewed direct political involvement but now felt it was important to keep the pressure on.

Even after Lincoln's Emancipation Proclamation was announced, Chapman remained dubious. It struck her as yet another half-measure. In particular, she objected to Lincoln's plan to compensate slave owners who remained loyal to the Union cause. "Think of it! Our grandchildren paying off Southern claims of this kind," she wrote. "[It] stinks in the nostrils of people."[339]

As the Civil War progressed, Chapman's spirits were buoyed by the progress made. Congress was advancing emancipation legislation, and Black troops were now playing a major role in the Union army and making gains in terms of pay and rank. She felt their voting power would play a pivotal role in ending the war. Blacks were being elected to southern union conventions, and new "Union Leagues" were spreading with a platform of immediate emancipation. "These are just a few of the signs of the times," she wrote hopefully to a friend at the end of 1863.[340]

Once the tide of the war had turned in the Union's favor, Chapman was surprised how quickly attitudes toward abolitionists began to change. After spending the winter holidays with her now grown son and his family in New York, she returned home to Weymouth and traveled into Boston for the day.

She described the reaction in January 1864. "I never saw such readiness to express regret and repentance for past complicity with slavery. The common formula was,—ah, you were right and we were wrong," she wrote to her daughter, adding that among her fellow abolitionists the general reaction was, "'We told you so!'"[341]

While some abolitionists remained skeptical of Lincoln and wanted to force him into repudiating southern amnesty efforts, Chapman's views on the president had come around. She disagreed with such "bullying" tactics and felt there was room in the abolitionist tent for differing views.[342] Increasingly, she seemed at peace, as the goal of her life's work to abolish slavery now seemed close at hand.

In 1865, after the Thirteenth Amendment was formally submitted to the states for ratification, Chapman attended an evening celebration in Boston with Garrison and other abolitionists. A massive crowd gathered at the Boston Music Hall, located less than half a mile from the old antislavery office, but the reception was far different than what they experienced thirty years earlier during the Gentlemen's Mob. This time, the state's governor and other political leaders were not only in attendance but on the same dais as Garrison, who was chosen to offer the keynote address. The program for the Grand Jubilee included prayers, music, hymns and a rousing rendition of "The Star-Spangled Banner."

Chapman appreciated the symbolism of Garrison serving as the featured speaker before so many Bostonians in broadcloth. She felt that he rose to the momentous occasion with his remarks. "I never heard Garrison so impressive. The great assembly seemed to be of one heart and one mind with him and cheers and weeping came from the deeps of their heart at every word he uttered," she wrote.[343]

The reaction to the news both at the event and more broadly in the city was exultant. Chapman described the firing of cannons and ringing of bells and strangers in the streets stopping to shake hands in jubilee. She knew there would be a new set of issues to overcome once slavery was formally abolished, but she was optimistic and felt the younger generation was up to the challenge. She believed that newly freed and enfranchised Black citizens could be a powerful check on the southern states and the "humiliated friends of the slave power."

"To show you how strong the current of righteousness I need only say that ambition, seeking for a political cry, finds none so popular as 'negro suffrage'!" she wrote to a British abolitionist friend.[344]

With its mission accomplished, the final edition of the *Liberator* rolled off the press on December 29, 1865. Chapman and her son jointly contributed

259. A few days earlier, he wrote to his wife and mentioned the chatter of a draft Garrison effort: "Nay, many talk of putting me on the list of representatives to the Legislature, to be chosen on Monday next. There is a strong reaction already in our favor, and the news from the interior is most encouraging." In the end, Garrison reportedly received eighty to ninety votes. See Garrison letter to Helen Garrison, November 7, 1835, as published in Merrill, *Letters*.

260. As reported in *Newburyport Morning Herald*, November 14, 1835, 2.

Chapter 19

261. James Alvord and Anna Grew got married a year later. Alvord practiced law in Greenfield and was later elected to Congress in 1839 but died before he could take office. He claims one other unusual fact which is that he was born in a town that no longer exists; Greenwich, Massachusetts, was subsumed to form the Quabbin Reservoir in 1938 and is now mostly under water.

262. Details on Ann Greene's introduction to Phillips and Sumner's demurral came from *Boston Sunday Post*, November 26, 1911, 31; Austin, *Life and Times*, 86; Sears, *Wendell Phillips*, 33–34; Pierce, *Memoir*, 164.

263. Sears, *Wendell Phillips*, 34.

264. It was rumored in August that Lyman would not run again and that Samuel Armstrong, the state's lieutenant governor, would step forward as the Whig nominee. See *Boston Investigator*, August 21, 1835, 2.

265. Lyman, *Memoir*, 28–29.

266. There are variations on the translation of the Latin phrase; this is how the *Liberator* translated. "Hancock" was Reverend Henry C. Wright. He later became a regular contributor to the *Liberator*.

267. *Liberator*, November 14, 1835, 2–3.

268. Garrison letter to Henry Benson, December 5, 1835, as published in Merrill, *Letters*.

269. Ibid.

270. Clarkson helped lead efforts to ban the trade of enslaved persons in Great Britain, including passage of the Slave Trade Act of 1807, and devoted his lengthy career to antislavery causes. Clarkson was of his grandfather's generation, and Garrison greatly admired him. During his trip to England in 1833, Garrison visited an aging and nearly blind Clarkson in the company of Nathan Paul, uncle of Susan Paul. The men met for over four hours at Clarkson's home in Ipswich, England. Clarkson had declared himself neutral on the issue of colonization, and both Garrison and Paul politely tried to persuade him to abandon that view and join them in opposition. See Second Annual Report of the Board of Managers, New England Anti-Slavery Society, presented January 15, 1834, 46–48.

271. Garrison's account read in pertinent part: "It is not true that I left either the building or the city because I was intimidated—but I left both at the earnest entreaty of the city authorities, and of several friends, and particularly on account of the delicate state of Mrs. Garrison's health." Her letter is referenced in a letter

from Garrison to his wife written the following week. See *Liberator*, November 7, 1835, 3; Garrison letter to Helen Garrison, November 14, 1835, as quoted in Merrill, *Letters*.

272. *Liberator*, November 14, 1835, 3.

Chapter 20

273. Martineau dated her hearing impairment to the age of twelve, and it grew progressively worse over time. It was not until her twenties, however, that she began using an ear trumpet. At times, she also used a rubber tube with a cup at one end for assistance. Martineau did not shy away from talking or writing about her disability. In her 1834 essay "Letter to the Deaf," she wrote openly of her experiences in the hopes of assisting others with significant hearing impairments. Martineau also used her deafness to her advantage on occasion and was known to demonstrate her displeasure with certain speakers by putting down her ear trumpet to indicate that she was done listening.

274. Chapman, *Harriet Martineau*, 345.

275. Martineau later acknowledged that her views were "half-informed."

276. In a letter to Isaac Knapp, Garrison colorfully described his encounter on the train that afternoon just before the women's meeting: "There were two ladies in our car—one a fat dowager-looking female—the other younger and less corpulent—probably mother and daughter. As we were stopping a few moments at Canton, a gentleman jokingly expressed his surprise to them, that they had not waited and attended the Ladies Anti-Slavery meeting that afternoon. 'Oh,' they said quite emphatically, 'we are not antislavery.' I wanted to say to them—but the fear of being thought impertinent kept me from intruding upon their conversation—'What! Not anti-slavery? Do you mean to say that you are in favor of slavery? Or what do you mean? If you are not antislavery, then you are for concubinage, pollution, robbery, cruelty; then you are for making merchandize of God's image, for setting aside the forms and obligations of marriage, for darkening the human intellect, and debasing the soul.'" See Garrison letter to Isaac Knapp, November 19, 1835, as published in Merrill, *Letters*.

277. Martineau, *Retrospect*, 151–58; and Chapman, *Harriet Martineau*, 345–53.

278. *Right and Wrong*, 1835, 73–74.

279. Martineau, *Retrospect*, 156.

280. It took a few days for news of Martineau's remarks to circulate, but once it did, the blowback was fierce, and her "indiscretion" was widely panned—except by the *Liberator* and a handful of abolitionist-friendly papers.

Chapter 21

281. Garrison, *Ann Phillips*, 5.

282. Ibid., 8.
283. Phillips, *Freedom Speech*, quoting letter from Sarah Southwick to John Latham on November 17, 1890.
284. *Boston Globe*, February 5, 1884, 1.
285. *Liberator*, October 19, 1855, 2.
286. Wendell Phillips Garrison was born on June 4, 1840.
287. Prior to being elected mayor, Smith was a doctor, author and amateur sculptor. During his tenure, Mayor Smith imported red and gray squirrels from Vermont and had them released on Boston Common. He also tried to sell Quincy Market, build a "lunatic asylum" on one of the Boston Harbor Islands and implement a tax on foreign visitors arriving in city ports. The squirrels remain, but few of his other plans worked out. See *Boston Herald*, January 1, 1855, 4; December 26, 1855, 4; *Massachusetts Spy*, May 27, 1855, 3; *Gleason's Pictorial*, vols. 6–7, F. Gleason Publisher, 1854, 64; Fahey, *Boston's 45 Mayors*, 13.
288. News was circulating that an ailing Jackson was notified by his doctor he had only a short time to live. Garrison shared the sad news in a letter to Maria Chapman on November 25, 1855, writing glowingly of his friend and calling him "one of the pillars of our anti-slavery temple." Jackson recovered from the unknown ailment and lived another six years.
289. *Liberator*, July 21, 1854, 2.
290. Frederick Douglass aptly summed up Garrison's talents in his eulogy: "As I now remember his speaking he was not as the phrase goes, an orator. There were no striking gestures, no fine flow of words, no dazzling rhetoric and no startling emphasis. His power as a speaker was the power which belongs only to manly character, earnest conviction, and high moral purpose." See Frederick Douglass, "Speech on the Death of William Lloyd Garrison," June 2, 1879, www.loc.gov/item/mfd.23012.
291. Wendell Phillips's eulogy of Garrison.
292. Yerrinton, *Proceedings*, 35.

Epilogue

293. *Zion's Herald*, as reprinted in *Liberator*, May 12, 1837, 3.
294. See Letter to Jonathan Phillips, Meltzer, Holland and Krasno, *Lydia Maria Child*, 583; and Grover and da Silva, "Historic Resource Study."
295. A book could be written on the philosophical divisions and political infighting that split the Boston Female Anti-Slavery Society, and it has. See Hansen, *Strained Sisterhood*, in bibliography.
296. The story of her catching ill on the steamboat trip comes from a recollection of Sarah Southwick. There is no independent confirmation of her story on record, but the facts generally comport with what we know about Paul's death from the *Liberator* notice and city death records (see subsequent note). Also, Southwick sat next to Paul during her last holiday fair and may have heard the story then. See Southwick, *Reminiscences*, 29.

297. Anne Warren Weston letter to Henry and Maria Chapman, May 5, 1841, BPL.

298. Southwick, *Reminiscences*, 29.

299. For details about Paul's participation in the holiday fair, see *Liberator*, February 25, 1840, 3; January 1, 1841, 3 (which includes floor diagram of the fair setup). Her death was reported in the *Liberator*, April 23, 1841, 3; and reprinted in *The Colored American*, May 8, 1841. According to City of Boston death records, she died of consumption on April 19, 1841, at the age of thirty-one and was buried at St. Matthew's Church in South Boston six days later. The newspaper death notices record her age as "about 32."

300. The *New York Whig* was the alleged culprit. See *Nantucket Inquirer & Mirror*, June 1, 1839, 2.

301. It was later named the Lyman School for Boys.

302. "Proceedings of the Dedication of the Fountain on Eaton Square," 36–42.

303. *Boston Sunday Budget*, "The Garrison Mob," March 18, 1883.

304. Ibid. See also Garrison and Garrison, *William Lloyd Garrison*, Vol. 2, 10–11.

305. Aaron Cooley letter to Garrison, July 22, 1866, BPL.

306. *Boston Daily Advertiser*, "Local Matters about Town," October 21, 1869, 1.

307. Francis Jackson Garrison letter, December 18, 1872, as published in Merrill, *Letters*, 61–62.

308. Garrison letter to John B. Vashon, July 27, 1847, as originally published in the *Journal of Negro History* 12, no. 1 (1927): 33–40.

309. *Waltham Free Press*, June 9, 1867, 1.

310. *The Index* (OH), October 22, 1870, 7, quoting *Boston Traveller*.

311. Chapman letter, December 19, [1859], BPL.

312. Phillips said later that he regretted the remark.

313. *Liberator*, February 26, 1864, 1.

314. *Liberator*, "Speech of Wm. Lloyd Garrison," May 19, 1865, 2.

315. Garrison letter to Wendell Phillips, January 1, 1866, as quoted in Merrill, *Letters*.

316. *New York World*, January 29, 1866, 4.

317. This was part of a lengthy series of resolutions read by Phillips and adopted by the American Anti-Slavery Society. See *New York Observer*, May 17, 1866, 6.

318. Martyn, *Wendell Phillips*, 372, quoting April 9, 1870 speech.

319. Address of Wendell Phillips, "The People Coming to Power!" delivered at Salisbury Beach (MA), September 13, 1871, published by Lee & Shepard, 1871.

320. *Boston Herald*, February 3, 1884, 1.

321. Ibid., February 12, 1884, 6, quoting state Senator Loring.

322. Newman went on to have a prominent career as an author and poet. Tribute published in *Christian Recorder* (TN), March 27, 1884, 1.

323. *Boston Herald*, February 13, 1884. 1.

324. Grimké, *Eulogy*.

325. Songs of the Free and Hymns of Christian Freedom. See announcement in *Liberator*, June 18, 1836, 3.

326. Higginson and Thacher, *Letters and Journals*, 9; Crawford, *Romantic Days*, 127, quoting stanza of poem by James Russell Lowell.

327. Anne Weston letter to Lucia Weston, September 28, 1840, BPL.

328. Her cause of death in city records is listed as "infantile" but is likely tuberculosis given the high incidents of it in the extended Chapman/Weston household.

329. Garrison could not resist drawing comparisons from the Philadelphia mob ("The city of brotherly love, forsooth!") to his own previous run-in. "The spirit of mobocracy, like the pestilence, is contagious; and Boston is once more ready to reenact the scenes of 1835," he wrote. See Garrison letter to George William Benson, May 25, 1838, BPL.

330. Anne Warren Weston letter to Mary Gray Chapman, May 23, [1838], BPL.

331. Lydia Maria Child letter to Caroline Weston, July 7, 1838, BPL.

332. *Liberator*, November 11, 1842, 3.

333. The letter was written in French. "Fasse le ciel qu'en revoyant votre pays vous y trouviez de nouvelle consolations, de noveaux encouragements, pour préserver dans la grande cause que vous avez adopté comme le but principal do votre vie." Nicholas Tourgueneff letter to Maria Chapman, September 29, 1855, BPL (note: this letter is incorrectly attributed to "Nikolaĭ Turgenev").

334. Garrison letter to Chapman, November 11, 1855, BPL.

335. Ibid.

336. *New York Tribune*, "Recollections of an Abolitionist," January 10, 1880, 2.

337. *Liberator*, October 9, 1857, 4.

338. Garrison letter to Oliver Johnson, August 9, 1860, BPL; Garrison letter to Oliver Johnson, October 7, 1861, BPL (copy).

339. Chapman letter to Elizabeth Bates Chapman Laugel, September 24, 1862, BPL.

340. Chapman letter to Mary Anne Estlin, December 29, 1863; Chapman letter to Anne Greene Chapman Dicey, June 12, 1863, BPL.

341. Chapman letter to Elizabeth Bates Chapman Laugel, January 17, 1864, BPL.

342. Chapman singled out Wendell Phillips as one of the abolitionists who appeared intent on bullying the government. See letter to Elizabeth Bates Chapman Laugel, February 23, 1864, BPL.

343. Chapman letter to Mary Anne Estlin, February 5, 1865, BPL.

344. Ibid.

345. Ibid.

346. John Jay Chapman, who later became a prominent writer, author and poet. See Howe, *John Jay Chapman*, 13.

347. Chapman letter to Elizabeth Pease Nichol, December 31, 1875, BPL.

348. Though fighting a bad cold, Garrison was in attendance and spoke for nearly an hour recounting the events of the day, including Chapman's now famous encounter with Mayor Lyman. Wendell Phillips, James Buffum, Samuel Sewall and Louisa May Alcott were among the one hundred or so antislavery activists also present. It is not clear why Chapman did not attend. See *Boston Journal*, October 22, 1878, 4.

349. Chapman letter to Samuel May, May 15, [1881], BPL.

350. Garrison letter to Wendell Phillips, November 1870, Blagden Collection, Harvard University.

351. Chapman letter to Samuel May, June 3, 1881, BPL.
352. Letter from Deborah "Dora" Weston to Anne Whitney, July 7, 1885, Wellesley College Archives, Anne Whitney Papers, repository.wellesley.edu/object/ wellesley12125. (Letter is incorrectly attributed to Maria Chapman.)
353. *Boston Journal*, "A Notable Gathering," April 23, 1886, 3.
354. *Boston Globe*, July 15, 1915, 6.

SELECTED BIBLIOGRAPHY

Austin, George Lowell. *Life and Times of Wendell Phillips*. Boston: Lee & Shepard Publishers, 1893.

Ayer, Mary Falwell. *Early Days on Boston Common*. Boston: Merrymount Press, 1910.

Barber, Samuel. *Boston Common: A Diary of Notable Events, Incidents and Neighboring Occurrences*. N.p.: Christopher Publishing House, 1916.

Bartlett, Irving H. "Wendell Phillips and the Eloquence of Abuse." *American Quarterly* 11, no. 4 (1959).

Baumgartner, Kabria. *In Pursuit of Knowledge: Black Women and Educational Activism in Antebellum America*. New York: New York University Press, 2019.

Benton, Josiah H., Jr. *A Notable Libel Case: The Criminal Prosecution of Theodore Lyman Jr. by Daniel Webster in the Supreme Judicial Court of Massachusetts November Term 1828*. N.p.: Charles E. Goodspeed, 1904.

Brown, Ira. "An Antislavery Agent: C.C. Burleigh in Pennsylvania, 1836–1837." *Pennsylvania Magazine of History and Biography* 105, no. 1 (January 1981).

Brown, Lois, ed. *Memoirs of James Jackson: The Attentive and Obedient Scholar Who Died in Boston October 31, 1833, Aged Six Years and Eleven Months, by His Teacher Miss Susan Paul*. Cambridge, MA: Harvard University Press, 2000.

———. "Out of the Mouths of Babes: The Abolitionist Campaign of Susan Paul and the Juvenile Choir of Boston." *New England Quarterly* 75, no. 1 (2002): 52–79.

Chambers, Lee V. *The Weston Sisters: An American Abolitionist Family*. Chapel Hill: University of North Carolina Press, 2014.

Chapman, Maria, ed. *Harriet Martineau's Autobiography*. Boston: Osgood and Company, 1877.

Cohen, Daniel A. "Passing the Torch: Boston Firemen, 'Tea Party' Patriots, and the Burning of the Charlestown Convent." *Journal of the Early Republic* 24, no. 4 (2004): 527–86.

Congdon, Charles T. *Reminiscences of a Journalist*. Boston: Osgood and Company, 1880.

Crawford, Mary C. *Romantic Days in Old Boston: The Story of the City and Its People During the Nineteenth Century*. Boston: Little, Brown, 1910.

Cromwell, Adelaide M. *The Other Brahmins: Boston's Black Upper Class 1750–1950*. Fayetteville: University of Arkansas Press, 1994.

Davis, William. *History of the Judiciary of Massachusetts, Including the Plymouth and Massachusetts Colonies, the Province of the Massachusetts Bay, and the Commonwealth*. Boston: Boston Book Company, 1900.

Drake, Samuel Adams. *Old Landmarks and Historic Personages of Boston*. N.p., 1876.

Emerson, Ralph Waldo. *Journals of Ralph Waldo Emerson, with Annotations*. Boston: Houghton Mifflin, 1909–14.

Fahey, Joseph, ed. *Boston's 45 Mayors: From John Phillips to Kevin H. White*. Boston: Boston City Record, 1975.

Garrison, Francis Jackson. *Ann Phillips, Wife of Wendell Phillips, a Memorial Sketch*. Cambridge, MA: Riverside Press, 1886.

Garrison, Wendell Phillips, and Francis Jackson Garrison. *William Lloyd Garrison, 1805–1879; The Story of His Life Told by His Children*. Vol. 2, *1835–1840*. New York: The Century Co., 1885.

Garrison, William Lloyd. *Helen Eliza Garrison: A Memorial*. Cambridge, MA: Riverside Press, 1876.

———, ed. *The Abolitionist: Or Record of the New-England Anti-Slavery Society*. Boston: printed by Garrison and Knapp, 1833.

Glasgow Ladies' Emancipation Society. *Three Years' Female Anti-Slavery Effort, in Britain and America: Being a Report of the Proceedings of the Glasgow Ladies' Auxiliary Emancipation Society, Since Its Formation in January*. N.p.: Aird & Russell, 1834.

Grimké, Archibald. *Eulogy on Wendell Phillips*. Boston: Rockwell and Churchill, 1884.

———. *William Lloyd Garrison, the Abolitionist*. New York: Funk & Wagnalls Co., 1891.

Grover, Kathryn, and Janine V. da Silva. Historic Resource Study, Boston African American National Historic Site, 2002. npshistory.com/publications/boaf/hrs.pdf.

Hammett, Theodore M. "Two Mobs of Jacksonian Boston: Ideology and Interest." *The Journal of American History* 62, no. 4 (1976): 845–68.

Hansen, Debra Gold. *Strained Sisterhood: Gender and Class in the Boston Female Anti-Slavery Society*. Amherst: University of Massachusetts Press, 1993.

Higginson, Thomas Wentworth, and Mary Potter Thacher. *Letters and Journals of Thomas Wentworth Higginson, 1846–1906*. Boston: Houghton Mifflin, n.d.

Horton, James. "Generations of Protest: Black Families and Social Reform in Ante-Bellum Boston." *The New England Quarterly* 49, no. 2 (1976): 242–56.

Horton, James, and Lois E. Horton. *Black Bostonians: Family Life and Community Struggle in the Antebellum North*. Rev. ed., New York: Holmes and Meier, 1979.

Howe, M.A. Dewolfe. *John Jay Chapman and His Letters*. Boston: Houghton Mifflin, 1937.

Hyde, Lynn E. "West Street: Nexus of Boston Reform, 1835–1845." Master's thesis, Harvard Extension School, 2018.

Jacobs, Donald M. "William Lloyd Garrison's *Liberator* and Boston's Blacks, 1830–1865." *The New England Quarterly* 44, no. 2 (1971): 259–77.

Jeffrey, Julie Roy. *The Great Silent Army of Abolitionism: Ordinary Women in the Antislavery Movement.* Chapel Hill: University of North Carolina Press, 2000.

Johnson, Oliver, and J. Greenleaf Whittier. *William Lloyd Garrison and His Times; or, Sketches of the Anti-Slavery Movement in America, and of the Man Who Was Its Founder and Moral Leader.* Boston: B.B. Russell & Co., 1880.

Levesque, George A. "Before Integration: The Forgotten Years of Jim Crow Education in Boston." *The Journal of Negro Education* 48 (Spring 1979): 113–25.

Lyman, Theodore, III. *Memoir of Theodore Lyman, Jr.* Cambridge, MA: J. Wilson and Son, University Press, 1881.

———, ed. *Papers Relating to the Garrison Mob.* Cambridge, MA: Welch, Bigelow and Co., 1870.

Marcus, Robert D. "Wendell Phillips and American Institutions." *The Journal of American History* 56, no. 1 (1969): 41–58.

Martineau, Harriet. *The Martyr Age of the United States.* Boston: Weeks, Jordan & Company, 1839.

———. *Retrospect of Western Travel.* London: Saunders and Otley, 1838.

———. *Society in America.* Vol. 1. London: Saunders and Otley, 1837.

Martyn, William Carlos. *Wendell Phillips: The Agitator.* New York: Funk & Wagnalls Company, 1890.

Massachusetts Legislature. House Reports. "Free Negroes and Mulattoes." No. 46. January 16, 1822.

Mayer, Henry. *All on Fire: William Lloyd Garrison and the Abolition of American Slavery.* New York: Norton & Company, 2008.

May, Samuel J. *Some Recollections of Our Antislavery Conflict.* Boston: Fields, Osgood, & Co., 1869.

Meltzer, Milton, Patricia G. Holland and Francine Krasno, eds. *Lydia Maria Child: Selected Letters, 1817–1880.* Amherst: University of Massachusetts Press, 1982.

Merrill, Walter, ed. *The Letters of William Lloyd Garrison.* Vol. 1: *I Will Be Heard.* Cambridge, MA: Harvard University Press, 1971.

Minot, William. *Mr. Minot's Address: Delivered at the Dedication of the Smith School House in Belknap Street, March 3, 1835.* Boston: Webster and Southard, Printers, Cornell University Library, n.d.

Mitchell, J. Marcus. *The Paul Family.* Boston: Society for the Preservation of New England Antiquities, 1973.

Morris, Christopher. "An Event in Community Organization: The Mississippi Slave Insurrection Scare of 1835," *Journal of Social History* 1 (1988): 93–111.

Nell, William Cooper. *The Colored Patriots of the American Revolution: With Sketches of Several Distinguished Colored Persons.* Boston: Robert F. Wallcut, 1855.

Ofenstein, Sharon K. *Old State House: Boston National Historic Park Historic Structure Report.* Boston: Society for the Preservation of New England Antiquities Consulting Services Group, 1977.

Oliver et al. "February Meeting, 1881. Tribute to Thomas Carlyle; Tribute to Professor J.L. Diman; The Garrison Mob; The Clark and Hutchinson Houses." *Proceedings of the Massachusetts Historical Society*, Vol. 18, 1880.

Phillips, Wendell. *The Freedom Speech of Wendell Phillips. Faneuil Hall, December 8, with Descriptive Letters From Eye Witnesses*. N.p.: Wendell Phillips Hall Association, 1891.

————. *Speeches, Lectures and Letters*. Boston: Lee & Shepard Publishers, 1884.

Pierce, Edward Lillie. *Memoir and Letters of Charles Sumner: 1811–1838*. Boston: Roberts Brothers, 1877.

"Proceedings of the Dedication of the Fountain on Eaton Square, Ward 24, October 24, 1885." Boston City Council. 1886.

Quarles, Benjamin. *Black Abolitionists*. Oxford: Oxford University Press, 1969.

Rice, C. Duncan. "The Anti-Slavery Mission of George Thompson to the United States, 1834–1835." *Journal of American Studies* (1968): 13–31.

Richards, Leonard L. *Gentlemen of Property and Standing*. Oxford: Oxford University Press, 1970.

Rich, Robert. "'A Wilderness of Whigs': The Wealthy Men of Boston." *Journal of Social History* 4, no. 3 (1971): 263–76.

Saillant, John. "'This Week Black Paul Preach'd': Fragment and Method in Early African American Studies." *Early American Studies* 14, no. 1 (2016): 48–81.

Sears, Lorenzo. *Wendell Phillips, Orator and Agitator*. New York: Doubleday Page and Co., 1909.

Southwick, Sarah H. *Reminiscences of Early Anti-Slavery Days*. Boston: Riverside Press, 1893.

Stewart, James Brewer. *Wendell Phillips: Liberty's Hero*. Baton Rouge: Louisiana State University Press, 1986.

Stimpson, Charles, Jr. *Stimpson's Boston Directory*. N.p., 1835.

Stowe, Harriet Beecher. *Men of Our Times: Leading Patriots of the Day*. Hartford, CT: Hartford Publishing Co., 1868.

Taylor, Anne-Marie. *Young Charles Sumner*. Amherst: University of Massachusetts Press, 2001.

Taylor, Claire. *Women of the Anti-Slavery Movement: The Weston Sisters*. New York: St. Martin's Press, 1995.

Tiffany, Nina Moore. *Samuel E. Sewall: A Memoir*. Boston: Houghton, Mifflin and Co., 1898.

Wigham, Eliza. *The Anti-Slavery Cause in America and Its Martyrs*. N.p.: A.W. Bennett, 1863.

Wightman, Joseph Milner. *Annals of the Boston Primary School Committee, from Its First Establishment in 1818, to Its Dissolution in 1855*. Boston: Rand & Avery, 1860.

Wilson, T.L.V. *The Aristocracy of Boston*. Boston, 1848.

Woodberry, George Edward. *Wendell Phillips: The Faith of an American*. N.p.: Woodbury Society. 1912.

Wyatt-Brown, Bertram. "The Abolitionists' Postal Campaign of 1835." *The Journal of Negro History* 50, no. 4 (1965): 227–38.

Yee, Shirley. *Black Women Abolitionists: A Study in Activism, 1828–1860.* Knoxville: University of Tennessee Press, 1992.

Yerrinton, J.M.W. *Proceedings of the Anti-Slavery Meeting Held in Stacy Hall, Boston, on the Twentieth Anniversary of the Mob of October 21, 1835.* N.p.: R.W. Wolcutt, 1855.

Yocum, Barbara. "Smith School House: Historic Structure Report." National Park Service, North Atlantic Region, 1998.

Zorn, Roman J. "The New England Anti-Slavery Society: Pioneer Abolition Organization." *The Journal of Negro History* 42, no. 3 (1957): 157–76.

INDEX

ABOUT THE AUTHOR

Josh S. Cutler is an attorney and state legislator representing the Sixth Plymouth District of Massachusetts. He currently serves as House chair of the Joint Committee on Labor and Workforce Development. A former newspaper editor, Cutler is a graduate of Skidmore College, Suffolk Law School and the University of Massachusetts at Dartmouth (MA, environmental policy). He is also the author of *Mobtown Massacre: Alexander Hanson and the Baltimore Newspaper War of 1812* (The History Press, 2019). When he's not hot on the trail of nineteenth-century abolitionist firebrands or Federalist agitators, Cutler enjoys photography, traveling, hiking and spending time with his children.

Visit us at
www.historypress.com

Chapter 20

LIBERTY'S BELL

My hopes are stronger than my fears.

S usan Paul walked the familiar route from her segregated Beacon Hill neighborhood across the Boston Common toward the home of Francis Jackson. It was a beautiful November afternoon, and she passed by the grand Hollis Street Church with its two-hundred-foot spire reaching for the sky, adorned with an elegant clock on its steeple.

A short four weeks ago—almost to the minute—she had made a similar journey to the antislavery office for the annual meeting of the Boston Female Anti-Slavery Society. Then, as now, she was apprehensive about what might happen, but like Maria Chapman, she remained committed to her mission. Harriet Martineau was also anxious about the meeting, though mostly for different reasons. The thirty-three-year-old British writer and intellectual first arrived in the United States in the fall of 1834. Martineau had a significant hearing impairment dating back to her youth and carried around a hearing trumpet to allow her to communicate more easily.[273] Perhaps as a result, she developed a keen sense of observation, and her insightful essays on politics and economics aimed at popular audiences earned her considerable notice on both sides of the Atlantic.

Martineau's visit to the United States was ostensibly for relaxation, but she also planned to continue her writing and research. She had written on the topic of slavery and considered herself an "English abolitionist" but wanted to learn more about the colonization and immediate emancipation movements from an American perspective and see the impacts of slavery in person. Martineau's extended journey took her through much of the South, and it was in Kentucky where she first received a fateful letter addressed to her from Boston. In an eloquent missive, the author made clear that she felt Martineau had been "blinded and beguiled by the slaveholders" on the issue of colonization and requested an audience to refute their claims and present the abolitionists' case.[274] Martineau was initially taken aback by the bold tone of the letter. "When I saw the signature 'Maria Weston Chapman,' I inquired who she was, and learned that she was one of the 'fanatics,'" she later admitted. The women continued their correspondence, and now, several months later, Martineau found herself in Boston with an invitation to the Boston Female Anti-Slavery Society meeting.

Harriet Martineau, NYPL.

During her luncheon with Chapman before the meeting, the conversation naturally turned to the topic of slavery. Martineau felt there could be no moral defense of slavery but thought that southern slaveholders were not entirely to blame, as many had grown up in prejudice and ignorance and had little choice in the matter. She also saw the pro-colonization movement as distinct from the proslavery position.[275] Chapman made it pointedly clear she did not share the same views and was determined to educate her new friend.

The luncheon was hosted at the home of Ellis G. Loring, an attorney and abolitionist who lived conveniently around the corner from Francis Jackson's house, where the women's meeting was to be held at three o'clock that afternoon. After their meal, Martineau walked up the stairs to retrieve her shawl, and Chapman approached holding her bonnet. "You know we are threatened with a mob again to-day," Chapman warned, "but I do not myself much apprehend it. It must not surprise us; but my hopes are stronger than my fears."

Martineau had already been warned of the prospects of another mob and understood the risk. Still, she found great inspiration and courage in Chapman's words. Her "clear silvery tones" had made an indelible impression.

circumstances she felt she had no choice but to break her silence and offer some comments. She rose slowly from her seat and spoke in a calm and dignified voice:

> *I have been requested by a friend present, to say something—if only a word—to express my sympathy in the objects of this meeting. I had supposed that my presence here would be understood as showing my sympathy with you. But as I am requested to speak, I will say what I have said through the whole South, in every family where I have been, that I consider slavery as inconsistent with the law of God, and as incompatible with the course of his Providence. I should certainly say no less at the North than at the South, concerning this utter abomination—and now I declare, that in your* principles, *I fully agree.*

Chapman listened carefully with her arms folded against her chest. She bowed her head as Martineau finished, and a look of satisfaction spread across her face. From her initial outreach via letter back in the spring to the society's meeting today, she had assiduously courted Martineau's support, knowing that her influential voice would greatly aid the abolitionist cause.

Martineau's remarks exceeded Chapman expectations, especially her audible emphasis on the word "principles." The subtle but notable inflection was as much a full-throated endorsement as the abolitionists could have hoped for, and the entire audience responded with a murmur of satisfaction. Martineau herself understood what she had just done, even if she had not really intended to make the emphasis. Her remarks would echo far beyond the four walls of the house. This was a bell that could not be unrung.[280]

Outside the house, the parcel of young men contributed occasional hoots and hollers and threw mud against the windows, but there was no further violence, and the crowd never exceeded thirty. Before the meeting concluded, the society elected officers for the next year, with Chapman, Parker and Paul all reprising their same roles, and then the women closed with a prayer and thanks to their host.

The annual meeting of the Boston Female Anti-Slavery Society was over—finally.

When it was time to attend the meeting, Martineau walked over with Loring and his wife. It was only a short distance, and they felt it was safer to be on foot than attract more attention with a carriage. Loring was ill but still determined to lend his support and escort the women safely. Garrison was not present, as he was traveling southbound on a train to rejoin his wife.[276]

To their relief, there was no large mob waiting to greet them on Hollis Street, just a dozen mischievous young men loitering by the front door of Jackson's stately home. The young men jeered at Susan Paul and the other Black women who climbed up the steps but did not take any further action. Once the women were all inside, the front door was bolted shut.

The prospects of a mob had not diminished attendance, and a large number of women arrived for the Boston Female Anti-Slavery Society meeting. Jackson made space by opening a folding door separating two large drawing rooms. By one count, there were 130 women in the two rooms, joined by the host and 2 other men who stood in the backyard just in case there was need to make a quick escape. Chapman sat by a small table in the middle with Mary Parker and the other society officers.[277]

The meeting got underway at half past three o'clock with a scripture reading and prayers. There was no juvenile choir on this occasion, but the women did join in singing an antislavery hymn. Martha Ball, the recording secretary, read her report, including a summary of the events from their eventful October meeting and then a series of resolutions that Chapman had drafted. The resolutions offered praise for Garrison and Thompson and gibes for the Boston establishment, interspersed with calls for Christian forgiveness.[278]

Martineau listened carefully, using her hearing aid for assistance. At one point, the woman sitting next to her leaned in, with a glance at Susan Paul and the other Black women in the audience, and asked if she felt uncomfortable "in assembly with people of color." Martineau replied that it made no difference to her. She had intended to sit through the meeting as an interested observer, rather than a participant, until she was passed a note from Ellis Loring handwritten on the back of the hymn note.

"Knowing your opinions, I just ask you whether you would object to give a word of sympathy to those who are suffering here for what you have advocated elsewhere," Loring asked. "It would afford great comfort."

Martineau was not pleased to be put on the spot. She knew the perils her countryman George Thompson had faced for his outspokenness, and she was not keen to assume his role; it could only lead to a formidable array of unpleasant consequences, she thought.[279] Still, as painful as it was, under the

"'There is great fear among the brethren and all the leaders are gone,'" Anne Weston lamented and wondered where she would now go to church.[220] Her sister attended services at the Free Church and was angered that there was not a single mention of the events of the past week. Even the regular monthly prayer concert, typically aimed at a broader antislavery audience, had to be canceled for want of a safe location to host it.

On Saturday, Chapman took a coach north of the city with three other abolitionists to check on George Thompson. His whereabouts were the subject of much speculation. According to one report, Thompson had left Boston and was hiding in New York, soon to sail for Liverpool, England. Another reported that he traveled to Newport, Rhode Island, and disguised himself in women's clothing to board a ferry to nearby Tiverton.[221]

The truth was less exciting. After leaving the city, he bounced around for several nights, staying in the homes of local abolitionists who were friendly to the cause. His arrival attracted attention at each stop, and he was chased out of town more than once. He was now staying near Salem, Massachusetts, and, according to Chapman, never appeared in better spirits. His presence had already caused a stir, however, and a local merchant offered a $100 bounty to anyone who caught him.[222]

Chapman and the abolitionists arranged for Thompson to quietly return to the city and stay at the home of Joseph and Thankful Southwick. It was apparent that the growing anti-abolitionist hostility was not confined to Boston and Thompson would not be much safer out in the country. At least in the city, it would be easier to hide him. Great pains were taken to keep his new location a secret, and only close friends knew the true name of the Southwicks' new houseguest.

Among them was Phillis Salem, the Southwicks' trusted house servant who had worked for the family for twenty-five years. Salem was also a member of the Boston Female Anti-Slavery Society, one of the few Black members who worked in a domestic role.[223]

While he was holed up, Thompson wrote a lengthy letter to Garrison that was later published in the *Liberator*. The letter, closer in length to a novella, was equal parts pep talk, diatribe and epistle. He cast the present climate for abolitionists in stark terms, noting the anti-abolition mania sweeping the city. "'Public opinion' is at this hour the demon of oppression," he wrote. "A MOB in BOSTON!! and such a mob!!! Thirty ladies *completely routed*, and a board 6 feet by 2 utterly demolished by 3000 or 4000 respectable ruffians— in broad day-light, and broad-cloth!"[224]

the abolitionists' antislavery views but nonetheless were well motivated to defend the cause of liberty. "There are individuals who boldly avow their determination to attend the next anti-slavery meeting fully equipped for military duty," he wrote.[214]

For the *Liberator*, the rioting did provide one financial benefit: a boost in subscription revenue. There was no advertising revenue to speak of, so the paper relied on subscription payments and generous patrons to stay afloat, and while the paper's voice was loud, the actual paid circulation was limited—especially among white residents of Boston. In fact, without the early support of Black readers, the paper might never have stayed afloat. After the first year, the paper reported four hundred four Black subscribers and fifty white ones. Readership grew over the next three years, but even after a concerted circulation campaign the previous winter, the *Liberator* still had fewer than three thousand subscribers.[215]

"I have been opposed to you, but I saw the dreadful proceedings yesterday and I am now convinced you have the truth on your side," one new subscriber wrote.[216] Another added, "Put down my name, for the *Liberator*. I thought till now, that I could not afford it, but I *can now*."[217]

The newspaper was delayed but did finally get printed and distributed on Monday, just two days behind schedule. ("Where the *Liberator* press is we can't tell but it is some where or other printing away," Chapman's sister reported to her aunt.)[218] Most of the published content predated the mobbing, but the new edition did have a lengthy narrative from Burleigh that offered the first real report of the incident from the abolitionists' perspective.

The reviews for the new issue were generally good; Garrison himself later voiced his approval when he was mailed a copy in Connecticut. Chapman's sister Anne, however, felt that Burleigh's account was too soft on the rioters and had not sufficiently framed the severity of the spectacle, though she was confident that Garrison would rectify that whenever he was able to return.

Chapman kept herself busy throughout the week and remained in good spirits despite the almost universal condemnation from the Boston establishment. Indeed, she appeared to welcome her newfound notoriety. "Maria continues to be in a state of great enjoyment. She receives such glory she can hardly bear it," her sister reported.[219]

The physical absence of Garrison and Thompson was certainly felt by the abolitionists, but so, too, was felt the moral absence of some ostensibly antislavery leaders. In particular, Chapman and her sisters were disappointed in the response from the city's religious leaders, most of whom fell silent rather than speak out contrary to the overwhelming public sentiment.

contrasting it to the present day. "What a change has been effected in public sentiment within twenty years! It has seemed to me in scanning the file of the *Liberator* for 1835, as if I were in another country, among another people," he said. "Our pathway is now, comparatively, strewed with flowers."

Garrison's belief in the sinfulness of slavery and his demand for immediate and unconditional emancipation remained core to his beliefs, and he was unwilling to cede an inch of ground, nor brook any disagreement. He did, however, admit that he had been wrong on one point, reflecting the hardening of his views over time. Proslavery forces often claimed that being antislavery also meant anti-Union, an argument that Garrison had once rejected but now came to believe must be true. A union that condoned slavery and was "cemented with the blood of millions in bondage" could not and should not be preserved, he felt.

"The sooner it is dissolved, the better," he told the assembled crowd. It was hardly a shocking statement from the man who just a year before, at a Fourth of July rally outside Boston, publicly burned a copy of the U.S. Constitution, calling it a "covenant with death."[289]

Wendell Phillips took to the floor following Garrison and a brief hymnal intermission. The two men's speaking styles reflected their own journeys over the past two decades. Garrison, driven by his powerful convictions, was steadfast and solid, known as a master agitator and writer but never a gifted orator.[290] The narrative arc of his own abolitionist views had changed little in substance over two decades. Other men ripen gradually, it was said, but Garrison came to his principles at a young age and never wavered.[291]

Phillips, on the other hand, was already a polished and effortless speaker, known for his plainspoken eloquence, conversational style and sharp wit. His speeches and lectures now attracted growing crowds who were both dazzled and antagonized by his oratory. Phillips's own abolitionist views were also dynamic, a fact that he readily acknowledged as he began his remarks. "At this hour, twenty years ago, I was below in the street—I thank God I am inside the house now," he said, and the crowd erupted in cheers.

Phillips focused much of his speech on the events of 1835, singling out Mayor Lyman for special criticism, both for his actions at the anti-abolition meeting and his inactions during the Gentlemen's Mob. "The mayor played a most shuffling and dishonorable part," he said.

By contrast, Phillips heaped high praise on the members of the Boston Female Anti-Slavery Society, pointing out a few of the women who were in the audience, including Thankful Southwick and Henrietta Sargent. He also invoked Maria Chapman's name—though she was not present—and retold a dramatized version of her run-in with Mayor Lyman. He credited the women and their bravery in standing up to the mob and overwhelming public opinion, as inspiration for his own conversion to the cause.

"My eyes were sealed, so that, although I knew the Adamses and Otises of 1776, and the Mary Dyers and Ann Hutchinsons of older times," he acknowledged, "I could not recognize the Adamses and Otises, the Dyers and Hutchinsons, whom I met in the streets of '35. These women opened my eyes."[292]

Much had changed since those days. Boston's gentlemen of property and standing were now far more likely to embrace the antislavery cause than to run from it—even if they might not all yet be ready to embrace Garrisonian-style abolitionism. The same could be said for most of the city's newspapers. Phillips's old law school friend Charles Sumner was no longer an awkward scholar buried in his legal books on Court Street but a United States senator jousting with southern slaveholders in the halls of Congress. Some faces like those of Mayor Theodore Lyman and Mary Parker had passed on, and others had burst on the scene. A nascent political movement was growing under a banner known as the Republican Party, and a more militant and violent antislavery strain was also emerging, portending armed struggles and internecine battles to come.

Still, despite all the progress of the antislavery movement, more than three million Americans remained enslaved, and Phillips, like Garrison, knew that challenging days lay ahead. Over the previous two decades, new proslavery states had been admitted to the Union and slave territory was extended in the west. Even in Boston, there remained a stubborn and outspoken thread of anti-abolitionist sentiment.

But change was possible. Maria Chapman and the women of Boston's Anti-Slavery Society had proven that. They had saved free speech for the city, Phillips told his audience, pointing out how their meeting today might not have even been possible twenty years ago. Every measure of Boston wealth and respectability stood in their path and yet, in the trial hours, these women, and a handful of men, faced the crucible and faced them down, he told the crowd. That must be the legacy of the Gentlemen's Mob.

"Let us not consent to be ashamed of the Boston of 1835. The howling wolves in the streets were not Boston. These brave...women were Boston," he boomed to roaring applause. "We will remember no other."

Chapter 21

HOWLING WOLVES

I thank God I am inside the house now!

Wendell Phillips left his home on Essex Street on a brisk Sunday afternoon in October. His wife, Ann, watched from their bedroom through a second-floor window where a narrow iron portico faced the street and offered a clear view of the bustling scene below. The modest three-floor house, an inheritance from Ann's late father, was surrounded by small shops, including a piano maker, a dentist and a provisions dealer. The woody scent of fine cut tobacco drifted from a nearby cigar and snuff shop.

Ann Greene Phillips's antislavery passions remained as vigorous as ever, but a debilitating illness kept her confined to the house and, most often, her bedroom. It had grown progressively worse since the couple was first married eighteen years ago, and both she and her husband accepted that it was now a permanent aspect of their lives together. Still, she took her illness in stride, good-humoredly referring to her husband as "my better three-quarters."[281]

Wendell Phillips walked east a block and then headed up Washington Street toward the old antislavery office, now known as Stacy Hall, where Maria Chapman and Susan Paul had held their fateful meeting twenty years ago to the day. He passed the Old State House where William Lloyd Garrison had been dragged by an anti-abolitionist mob and then delivered to the Leverett Street Jail by Mayor Theodore Lyman and his men.

Phillips, circa 1855. *Smithsonian.*

A new modern jail had since been built on Charles Street, and the mayor's office had moved to a larger space at the county courthouse. The Old State House now housed a variety of commercial tenants, including a telegraph office and tailor shop. City streets, once made from compressed gravel or dirt, now featured cobblestone and granite blocks, and gas streetlights, which had been a novelty, were now commonplace. New metal railways for horsecars began to appear on roadways, and an aqueduct and reservoir system now delivered an ample supply of fresh water into the city (thanks in part to the foresight of Mayor Lyman.)

As Phillips departed to make his return to the site for another abolitionist meeting, he might have heard his wife's well-known admonition: "Don't shilly-shally, Wendell!"[282] But there was little worry of that today. The city of Boston had certainly changed—growing significantly in both population and physical size over two decades—but he had changed even more.

Wendell Phillips would be no spectator today. If there was a single moment that evinced his formal conversion as an abolitionist, it came shortly after he was married—and, coincidentally, involved a mob.

On the evening of November 7, 1837, a proslavery mob mobilized against an antislavery newspaper in Alton, Illinois. Editor Elijah Lovejoy valiantly tried to defend the building where his printing press was stored and was shot five times and killed in the process. Lovejoy's violent death sparked a wave of indignation around the country, and nowhere more so than in Boston.

A public meeting was called at Faneuil Hall in early December and attracted a standing-room-only crowd of several thousand, including many who did not necessarily agree with the abolitionists but saw Lovejoy's death as an attack on free press and free speech. Others were less sympathetic, and the audience—nearly all men, save Maria Chapman and a handful of women in the gallery—reportedly included a "large mobocratic element."

Following introductions, a lengthy list of resolutions was read denouncing the attack on Lovejoy. The first few speakers stuck to the script and spoke out against the mob violence, but then the state's attorney general, James Austin, rose, red-faced, and passionately spoke out against the resolutions.